Page 45

D0914913

DATE

Lessons on Security
and Disarmament

FROM THE HISTORY OF THE
LEAGUE OF NATIONS

Lessons on Security and Disarmament

FROM THE HISTORY OF THE

LEAGUE OF NATIONS

BY

JAMES T. SHOTWELL

Acting President, Carnegie Endowment for
International Peace

AND MARINA SALVIN

Lecturer in Government, Barnard College

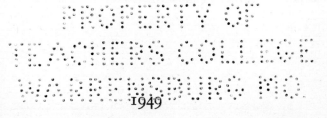

1949

PUBLISHED FOR THE CARNEGIE ENDOWMENT FOR
INTERNATIONAL PEACE
BY KING'S CROWN PRESS, NEW YORK

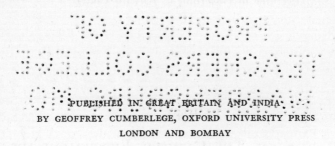

Preface

WHILE HISTORY never repeats itself, it comes very near doing so when the issues at stake are substantially the same. The ways for solving problems may vary, but even then the experience of the past often furnishes guides which neither statesman nor student of international affairs can ignore with impunity. The common idea that all of the effort connected with the League of Nations was more or less futile is utterly wrong and misleading, and it is time that some of the problems which were dealt with so seriously and at such great length by the statesmen at Geneva should be explored, not only for their historical interest, but for their practical bearing upon the work of the United Nations.

It is for this practical purpose that the following studies have been made, not merely to satisfy historical interests in the way in which the League of Nations worked, but to draw from that unique experiment suggestions and ideas which may be of use in the immediate or remote future. The points covered are, therefore, chosen with reference to discussions already being carried on in the Assembly of the United Nations and its associated organs of investigation and planning.

In the preparation of the text I am happy to have had the collaboration in research of Miss Marina Salvin, Lecturer in Government at Barnard College, who also prepared the Survey of Security Disputes in Part II of the study. The detailed section on the Ethiopian War in Part III was written by Mr. Robert K. Webb, University Fellow in History at Columbia University.

J. T. S.

New York City
January, 1949

Contents

I. METHODS AND INSTRUMENTS   1

   1. A COMPARISON OF THE COVENANT WITH THE CHARTER   1

   2. ARMAMENTS AS A CAUSE OF WAR   10

   3. THE LEAGUE TURNS TO THE PROBLEM OF SECURITY   16

   4. THE TREATY OF MUTUAL ASSISTANCE AND THE AMERICAN PLAN   20

   5. THE PROTOCOL OF GENEVA   24

   6. THE TREATIES OF LOCARNO   27

   7. PROPOSALS TO ORGANIZE PEACE   31

   8. THE TREATY TO DEVELOP THE MEANS FOR PREVENTING WAR   40

II. A COMPREHENSIVE SURVEY OF SECURITY DISPUTES BEFORE THE COUNCIL   45

III. MANCHURIA AND ETHIOPIA   81

   1. THE MANCHURIAN INCIDENT   81

   2. THE ETHIOPIAN WAR   92

APPENDIX   111

   RESOLUTION XIV OF THE THIRD ASSEMBLY   111

   PROTOCOL FOR THE PACIFIC SETTLEMENT OF INTERNATIONAL DISPUTES (1924)   113

   PACIFIC SETTLEMENT OF INTERNATIONAL DISPUTES, GENERAL ACT (1928)   125

   CONVENTION TO IMPROVE THE MEANS OF PREVENTING WAR (1931)   139

   REGULATIONS UNDER ARTICLE 4 OF THE CONVENTION TO IMPROVE THE MEANS OF PREVENTING WAR   144

I

Methods and Instruments

1. A COMPARISON OF THE COVENANT
WITH THE CHARTER

THE STARTING POINT for this study is, of course, a comparison of the Covenant of the League with the Charter of the United Nations. Without going into detail, there is one fundamental difference which stands out especially in the provisions for security. The Charter is more definite than the Covenant, a point which the makers of the Charter held to be greatly in its favor. The history of these past years, however, has by no means justified this theory, for the more definite the text the harder it is to fit it into all the varied and unforeseen circumstances in the vast range of international relations, and the easier it is for a legalistic minority to object. This problem of the rigid text is only too well known now because of the emphasis upon it of the Union of Soviet Socialist Republics. Many times in discussion, it has been pointed out that at San Francisco we did not expect that a veto would be used in any but a few rare instances where the vital interests of a nation were at stake. But if the minority had no other means of preventing an action which seemed to it to disregard its interests, the technical points were bound to be adduced in order to block action.

This is of vital importance in all planning for a more effective world organization. The idea that the United Nations could be strengthened by binding its members to legal obligations that are stricter and more far-reaching than those in the Charter of the United Nations is proceeding along the very line which strengthens the hand of the objector by offering him more points on which to object. Instead of insisting upon an ironclad system of obligations in what has been termed "the rule of law," those who would

1

strengthen the Charter should turn from the legalistic to the political possibilities. The structure of the United Nations should not be thought of in terms of courts and police, but of adjustment to changing realities. The courts and police should be there as well, but entirely subordinate to the political instrumentalities.

This at least is the outstanding lesson from the history of the League of Nations. It experimented with both the legalistic and political safeguards of peace and, without discounting the importance of binding obligations, realized more and more the fundamental fact which the British persistently advocated in Geneva, that the means for dealing with the current problems must be adjustable to the problems themselves. In short, the evolution of the League of Nations was the very opposite of that which relies upon hard and fast constitution.

This fundamental trend of the League of Nations has never been fully understood in American public opinion. One of the reasons for this misunderstanding of League history is that in the debates over the Covenant, both in Congress and throughout the country, attention was concentrated upon Article 10, which was the one most definite obligation. This was the article in which the Members of the League undertook "to respect and preserve as against external aggression, the territorial integrity and political independence of Members of the League." The article was Wilson's own, and was indeed the starting point for his conception of a world-wide League. It was an effort to state the Monroe Doctrine in terms applicable to the world at large and thus bring the experience of the United States in the Americas to the safeguarding of peace elsewhere. The Article, however, had a strangely paradoxical history, for in the United States the opponents of the Covenant regarded it as a dangerous extension of American obligations which would result in a freezing of the *status quo* throughout the world. On that ground it was the chief obstacle to the acceptance of the Covenant, although other articles were also attacked in the Senate debate. On the other hand, the European nations knew little and cared less about the history of the Monroe Doctrine. Even in the course of the Paris Peace Conference, ignorance concerning this century-old development of American foreign policy was freely expressed by even the delegates of major powers. The European peace system had rested, not upon any such unilateral guarantee as this, but upon the more adjustable—if apparently more hazardous—basis of the balance of power among many nations. Now for the balance of power was to be substituted collective security, but not necessarily for the maintenance of the strict territorial settlement of the Versailles Treaty. Therefore, Article 10 went into the discard and the League fell back upon an article which gave it greater liberty of action in the preservation of peace and, therefore, greater chance of success. This was Article 11 of the Covenant, which opened the door to the political as over against arbitral or legal settlement of disputes. This article turned out to be the most important one in the actual application of the Covenant, and yet in the Peace Conference negotiations no one paid much attention to it as it was regarded as a more or less obvious statement of the purpose and general character of the League, and in the debates in the American Senate no one paid any serious attention to it. Apparently it seemed to state commonplace generalities; in reality it opened the door to League action in the whole wide field of politics.

The text of Article 11 ran as follows:

1. Any war or threat of war, whether immediately affecting any of the Members of the League or not, is hereby declared a matter of concern to the whole League, and the League shall take any action that may be deemed wise and effectual to safeguard the peace of nations. In case any such emergency should arise the Secretary-General shall on the request of any Member of the League forthwith summon a meeting of the Council.

2. It is also declared to be the friendly right of each Member of the League to bring to the attention of the Assembly or of the Council any circumstance whatever affecting international relations which threatens to disturb international peace or the good understanding between nations upon which peace depends.

Nothing else in the Covenant of the League was so revolutionary in content as the opening sentence of this Article, and nothing in the procedure of the League was more effective than its apparently vague call to action. It is only against the background of history that the full import of the Article can be realized. Recourse to war was a sovereign right within the national state system which was the product of the whole long evolution of European history. That right was still recognized in the Covenant itself for it stated that in case all efforts to secure a pacific settlement of a dispute failed, then the Members of the League reserved to themselves "the right to take such action as they shall consider necessary for the maintenance of right and justice" (Article 15, section 17), the formula of diplomacy which means in other words that the nations reserve the right to go to war with each other as a last resort. Here we have what came to be known later as the hole in the Covenant by which the tides of war might sweep through what was otherwise intended to be the solid bulwark of enduring peace.

It was, therefore, essential that the Council of the League, as its executive organ, should be on the watch against "any war or threat of war," and should be ready to "take any action that may be deemed wise and effectual to safeguard the peace of nations."

The phrase "any action" was a grant of general powers which was not repeated in the Charter of the United Nations in its provisions for action by the Security Council. On the contrary, the Security Council of the United Nations is granted specific powers for the discharge of those duties laid down in the chapters on the pacific settlement of disputes, action with respect to threats to the peace and regional arrangements and trusteeship (cf. Article 24, section 2). Each of these functions is fairly clearly defined, far beyond any clarity of definition in the Covenant of the League. It is true that Articles 12 to 16 of the Covenant outlined the procedure for the pacific settlement of disputes and the sanctions for the maintenance of peace. But Article 11, which we are here considering, was held in reserve behind all the methods outlined for the pacific settlement of disputes or the sanctions, and gave the League a freedom of action for either the Assembly or the Council to deal realistically with the issues of war and peace.

The value of Article 11 was already seen at the first meeting of the Council of the League in dealing with the first of all disputes which came before it, that over the possession of the Aaland Islands, a dispute between Finland and Sweden. The pacific settlement of this dispute, in 1921, was admittedly largely due to the generous and statesmanlike attitude of Sweden, but it resulted in a real achievement for the League on the very threshold of its history.

A similar success was registered in the Mosul dispute between Great Britain and Turkey, and in the Upper Silesian dispute between Germany and Poland, the details of which do not concern us here, because in neither case was there a menace of war. But in October, 1925, a dispute arose between Greece and Bulgaria in which the threat of a Balkan war was actually stopped on the very verge of belligerency.

In October, 1925, Greek forces crossed the Bulgarian-Macedonian frontier and at once the Bulgarian Government sent in an appeal to the League of Nations. It was a weekend and some of the leading officials of the League were away, thus losing several hours during which the Greek invasion was proceeding. This point must be mentioned because it brought up at once the importance of having quick action to meet an emergency. Within an hour after receipt of the appeal, M. Aristide Briand, as Chairman of the Council, telegraphed to Sofia and Athens exhorting both parties to cease further action and withdraw their troops behind their own frontiers. The Council was summoned at once to meet in Paris, and it met three days later, members coming by airplane so as to lose no time. At the Council meeting, the Greek Government, not having replied as yet, was given an ultimatum of twenty-four hours for an unconditional order for withdrawal of its troops to Greek soil.

The action of the Council, which followed along the lines of its previous procedure, was to create a Commission of Inquiry which should go to the Macedonian frontier. For this purpose and in order to gain time, it "requested" Great Britain and Italy to send to Macedonia such officers as they had within reach and to keep the Council informed of the military situation.

Having thus secured a truce, the Council then appointed a Commission of Inquiry to investigate the whole situation, decide where the responsibility lay and indicate the terms of settlement. The Commission reported in due time, in the course of the following winter, and its Report was adopted by the Council and carried out by the disputing Governments. The incident was closed by the Greeks paying a heavy fine. Thus the League had succeeded in stopping a recognized aggression after the initial overt act had been committed. The League had been justified as an instrument for the preservation of peace between small powers; the question remained whether it would be equally successful when a Great Power was involved.

In judging the efficiency of the Council of the League in the application of Article 11, it must be kept in mind that political issues are frequently psychological and that the personalities of the statesmen who are responsible for securing settlement are fully as important as the institutions or instruments of settlement. The personal ascendency of M. Briand in Europe at the time of the Bulgar-Greek dispute was of the greatest importance. In a way he became the impersonation of the ideal of pacific settlement and he raised the moral prestige of the League so long as he was Chairman of the Council or a member of it. But this is only one instance of the general fact that in the middle 1920's the meetings of the Council were attended, not by deputies of governments, but by responsible ministers in power at the time. This gave a prestige to the Council which raised it above any other organ in European politics, a situation which was vitiated in the first instance by Mussolini and then by the skepticism of the conservative leaders in English politics who never had any faith in collective security.

It would carry us too far afield at this point to attempt even to outline the history of the action of the Council of the League of Nations under Article 11. We must leave for a later chapter the way in which it met the crises when "war or the threat of it" developed in Manchuria, in Spain, in Ethiopia and in central Europe. There is, however, one interesting episode, of less tragic import, but none the less of real significance, which is not well known and which definitely falls within this part of our narrative. This was the use of the procedure of conciliation by the Council itself in dealing with a dispute between France and Germany which arose in the spring of 1927, over the policing of the Saar Valley.

It will be recalled that in the Treaty of Versailles, Article 45 provided that "as compensation for the destruction of the coal mines in the north of France and as part payment towards the total reparation due from Germany for the damage resulting from the war, Germany cedes to France in full and absolute possession . . . the coal mines situated in the Saar Basin."

Similarly in Article 49 of the Treaty of Versailles, Germany renounced "in favor of the League of Nations, in the capacity of trustee, the government of the territory defined above. At the end of fifteen years from the coming into force of the present treaty, the inhabitants of the said territory shall be called upon to indicate the sovereignty under which they desire to be placed."

This regime of the Saar Valley was doubly resented by Germany because of the dominance of France in the government of the Saar Valley itself under the trusteeship of the League of Nations. This matter came to a head in the spring of 1927. Germany had been admitted to membership in the League in 1926 and one of the first questions which it raised was that of the French troops maintained as a police force in the Saar Valley. It insisted that this force of 800 men should be cut down to not more than 500.

This was the technical matter under dispute but it was brought up on a purely political basis. The German newspapers carried on a campaign against the "disguised military occupation of the Saar Valley by the French." The French newspapers replied against the effort by Germany to deny it the necessary means for "maintaining law and order in a turbulent population." The issue thus became one of good faith and political trust and not merely a question of 300 men. No better example was ever furnished of the difference between a juristic issue and a political dispute.

The question came up before the meeting of the Council of the League in March, 1927. The procedure was at first confined entirely to fact-finding, with reports from the League's officials in the Saar Valley as well as from French and German witnesses. This, however, could not reach the heart of the problem which was the charge on the part of the Germans that the French were misusing their trusteeship and the charge on the part of the French that the Germans were creating an issue in order to secure a change in regime. So hot and so difficult did the issue become that it was understood by both the French and the German delegations at Geneva that there was grave danger of Germany's giving up membership in the League unless sufficient concessions were made to it, while, on the other hand, M. Briand's Government would have fallen overnight if the settlement were of a kind that would look like a surrender to German pressure at Geneva.

At the close of a long day's dispute, in which it was apparent that no settlement was being reached, Vittorio Scialoja, the Italian member of the Council, found a formula which all could accept. It was, however, not a formula which any arbitral tribunal could have accepted, because it was a purely political compromise, arranged primarily for the purpose of saving the face of two governments, those of Gustav Stresemann and M. Briand, both of which were anxious to avoid a break but neither of them in a position to yield. Scialoja's compromise was that France could have its 800 police, but would make arrangements so that it would never show more than 500 of them at any one time.

Technically, this settlement seems trivial to the point of absurdity, and so it was apparently viewed by the American press, for little or no attention was paid to the incident in the United States. But in Europe, that session of the Council of the League was regarded as one of the most important instances of the value of conciliation. A hundred journalists watched all day long for the news that would reach one hundred million readers if perchance the dispute was not settled, that with Germany's withdrawal from the League the whole system of collective security was in the discard.

This incident is worth careful study for all further procedures of conciliation. It brings out more clearly than anywhere else in the history of that device that the political issue differs from an arbitral one in that the real points in dispute become less important than the state of mind in one nation with reference to another. The charge of bad faith is a far more serious thing than the question of

300 police. The poison that lies in such a charge can only be removed by lessening the importance of the issue itself through a recognition of the fact that agreement is more important than the claim of either disputant.

2. ARMAMENTS AS A CAUSE OF WAR

WHEN THE LEAGUE of Nations was founded no one anywhere doubted that the race in armaments had been largely responsible for the first World War. Therefore, "disarmament" was the largest single item in the peace movement of that time, and there was universal agreement that the first and greatest test of the League of Nations would be its ability to carry out a "reduction and limitation of armaments," which was the more cautious expression for the popular term, disarmament. The emphasis upon the problem of armaments was a somewhat belated development of the industrial revolution. It began in the second half of the nineteenth century with the transformation of the steel industry (Bessemer and open-hearth processes), with the building of iron-clad warships and the other military equipment produced by the heavy industries of Germany and France as well as of Great Britain. It was to check this race in armaments that the Hague Conferences were called in 1899 and 1907. The failure of these Conferences to lessen either the financial burden of increasing armaments or the apparent menace of them was followed by an increase in the armament race, especially after Great Britain had developed the dreadnought. Germany's acceptance of the apparent challenge was widely regarded as one of the steps which led toward the catastrophe of 1914. It was, therefore, inevitable that the League of Nations would at the very outset undertake to make good the disarmament clause of the Covenant (Article 8): "The members of the League recognize that the maintenance of peace requires the reduction of national armaments to the lowest point consistent with national safety and enforcement by common action of international obligations." The Article then calls upon the Council to formulate plans at least every ten years "for the consideration and action of the several Governments." These plans are to take into account "the geographical situation and circumstances of each state," but once adopted by the several Governments "limits of armaments therein fixed shall not be exceeded without the concurrence of the Council." Finally, the League members "undertake to exchange full and frank information as to the scale of their armaments, their military, naval and air programs and the condition of such of their industries as are adaptable to war-like purposes."

This Article of the Covenant was the basis for the long and apparently futile effort of the League of Nations to secure a general treaty for the reduction and limitation of armaments. Unfortunately, popular opinion concentrated upon the ultimate failure of the Disarmament Conference and has not realized even yet the extent to which the Geneva studies really clarified the problem, so that the United Nations need not repeat the mistakes of the early days, but on the contrary can profit from plans and proposals which though never put into practice embodied the experience and the practical wisdom of almost a generation of European statesmen.

The following study, based for the most part upon a survey of the documents, deals with this chapter of almost forgotten history, but before entering upon it, we should examine in the light of pre-war history, the fundamental assumption which underlay this movement, namely, that the race in armaments was largely responsible for the first World War.

The outlines of this history are sufficiently well known that we need not delay over the details. The first British dreadnought was built in 1905, at the instigation of the First Sea Lord of the Admiralty, Lord Fisher. This vessel, with its increased range of gunfire and torpedoes, its heavy armor and its steam turbines, introduced a new era in naval armament. It was inevitable that Germany would respond to this challenge and begin the building of the fleet in which it had been very weak previously. The German Navy League carried on propaganda of an extreme nationalist type, which fitted in with military propaganda for a larger "place in the sun." The growth of

German military potential in its fast developing industry was also an element in the growing feeling of insecurity on the part of its neighbors. In short, the new armament situation gave a new turn to the political basis of security, the balance of power. The French-Russian Alliance of 1894 was an almost direct result of the passage of the German Military Bill which increased the size of the German army. And in 1899, just after the meeting of the first Hague Conference, it was extended to provide for the maintenance of the balance of power as well as the maintenance of peace. During all of this period, however, England had maintained a policy of "splendid isolation." But the growing power of Germany was not materially altered, so far as Europe was concerned, by England's acceptance of an alliance with Japan in 1902. Two years later, however, in 1904, Great Britain and France achieved a complete diplomatic revolution in the formation of the *Entente Cordiale,* an expression of friendship between the two nations which for most of their history from beyond the days of Joan of Arc, had been either at war or in a state of indifferent peace.

The reason for this diplomatic revolution, however, was not to be found in the race in armaments but in the new imperialist policy of Germany which showed itself in the plans for the Berlin to Bagdad Railway, the German direction of the Turkish armies and hostility to French-British arrangements in the Mediterranean.

This and the Balkan ambitions of Austria disturbed by the Turkish-Balkan War of 1910, and not the race in armaments in itself, led directly to the outbreak of the first World War. There was, however, a real menace to peace in the growth in armaments, but it was due less to technical, purely military and naval developments, than to an extension of a military class, especially in Continental countries. The danger to peace and to democratic institutions of government by the growth of this class was most strongly felt in France. It had come to light in the Dreyfus case, which changed the slogan of French democracy from a fear of clericalism to a fear of militarism. This was best brought out by Jean Jaures in his effort to eliminate militarism from the French army in the plan known as *l'Armée Nouvelle.* It was his advocacy of reforms like this which

led to his assassination at the opening of the first World War. This
trend in the history of the Third Republic has never been sufficiently
appreciated outside of France. The Dreyfus case marked a turning
point away from the militaristic traditions which had been so largely
dominant in the great eras of French history, and the French radical
and social movements led European opinion throughout the first
decade of the twentieth century in anti-imperialist and antimilitarist
policies.

Unfortunately, however, French policy was confronted at almost
every turn by German opposition, frequently expressed in irritating
incidents which, whatever their real purpose, had the effect of rous-
ing French nationalism and rendering more difficult the pacific
policies of the Government. This was the situation in 1914, and it
explains both the relative unpreparedness of the French and the universal deeply felt conviction that militarist Germany was the
aggressor. For the contrast between the attitude of the French reserv-
ists and those called to the colors in Germany was so strong as not to
escape even the most superficial observer. Militarism is not only pride
in the strength of army or navy; it is also a readiness to use war as
the instrument of national policy, and it is this latter aspect of it
which is by all means the most important element. In this regard
German history as taught in the schools and colleges was as responsible for Germany's action in 1914 as the possession of a
powerful army.

German militarism was in contrast, not only with the relatively
pacific trend of Republican France, but also with the trend in other
democratic freedom-loving countries. This fact was obscured by the
universal acceptance of nineteenth-century political philosophy that
war was the final argument between nations and that the right to
go to war was the test of sovereignty itself. It was Woodrow Wilson
who clarified the issue, not only for America, but for all the world, by
insisting that American participation in the war was for the purpose
of ending war itself. This slogan of 1917 was soon destined to become the byword of disillusionment, as the magnitude of the task
became apparent and the intellectual and spiritual mobilization for

peace proved utterly unable to hold back the forces of nationalism in the "dark twenties."

Nevertheless, the treaties of peace with Germany and her allies embodied this purpose of Woodrow Wilson in two major provisions: those enforcing disarmament on the conquered nations, and the erection of the League of Nations which should act in place of armament rivalries as a guarantee of peace through provision for collective security.

The history of the armament control of Germany lies outside the field of this survey. But it should be recalled that it was only by inspection on the spot that the Allied Powers were able to secure any genuine measure of disarmament. The estimate which Marshal Ferdinand Foch made at the Armistice of the extent of German armaments was only one fifth of the amount which the Control Commission actually destroyed, and in later years there was even criticism of the inadequacy of the inspection itself.

Part V of the Treaty of Versailles, which dealt with the disarmament of Germany, also implied, although in vague, general and one might almost say quibbling terms, that the Allied and Associated powers would follow up Germany's disarmament with similar measures of their own. The preamble to this section of the Treaty read as follows: "In order to render possible the initiation of a general limitation of the armaments of all nations, Germany undertakes strictly to observe the military, naval and air clauses which follow." The drafters of this clause must surely have been aware of the fact that treaties dealing with such vital matters as security and armaments need to be precise and definite in their obligations; for the military authorities are bound to consider it to be their duty to save for their country as much freedom of action as they can. Therefore, the vague phrase implying an intention on the part of the Allied and Associated powers to proceed to a general limitation of the armaments of all nations was never taken seriously by the German military leaders who were forced to comply with rigid and exact provisions for the reduction of their armaments.

It was this situation which made the action of the League of Nations in the control of armaments so all-important, because the

whole issue was formally referred to it at the very beginning of its history. As Germany was not yet a member of the League, the drama which was unfolded at Geneva began as an effort to make good the moral obligation in the peace treaties. But Germany's absence from the League did not mean its absence from disarmament discussions. Even when it was not represented on commissions or committees, it remained for all Western Europe the heart of the armament problem.

3. THE LEAGUE TURNS TO THE PROBLEM

OF SECURITY

THE COUNCIL of the League, at its very first meeting, even before the Assembly had met, established a Permanent Military, Naval and Air Commission. This was in fulfillment of Article 9 of the Covenant which stated that "a Permanent Commission shall be constituted to advise the Council on the execution of the provisions of Articles 1 and 8 and on military, naval and air questions generally." The membership of this Commission as actually set up by the Council was appointed by the states represented by the Council from the military experts connected with their general staffs. The purpose of this method of appointment was that the Permanent Commission should be in touch with the military authorities back home on the ground that its action would be purely technical and, therefore, could be divorced from all questions of policy, which belonged to the civilian branch of the Government. The logic of this arrangement was obvious. But it worked out differently from what had been intended. For professional soldiers could hardly be expected to think in terms of any radical reduction of national armaments, and the more technical the questions became the more difficult they were to solve along any line of comparative ratios.

From the standpoint of those interested in the actual reduction of armaments the Permanent Commission was never regarded in any other light than that of an obstacle to the securing of any positive results. The criticism was perhaps not fully justified because the Council of the League did not in the early years offer policies in the fulfillment of which the Commission would have had to work definitely at its problem. In this regard the structure of the League was obviously unfortunate. In the history of the national state it has been an axiom that the military establishment should be merely the instrument for carrying out policies, and that militarism can develop fully as much under inadequate political control as under the militaristic trend of the civil government. This was never more clearly seen than in the case of Bismarck's dealings with the Prussian general staff. Although no statesman ever used the military arm with greater effect, Bismarck never yielded to von Roon or von Moltke the political decisions upon which military action rested. The weakness of the League was, therefore, more in the lack of agreed purpose in the Council than in the limitation of the Permanent Commission to a purely technical membership. But again the Council of the League could not be expected to have clear-cut directives for its technical body until the political situation had been clarified and the League's own strength for the maintenance of peace more definitely tested. In short, in the early pioneering years of the League of Nations the problem of armaments proved too complicated to be solved by any simple device such as the erection of a committee of military men to advise the Council on questions of security.

At the very first Assembly the situation began to be clarified because the Assembly established its commission alongside that of the Council. While in no way criticizing the Council's action, it set up a new body composed of civilian as well as military members to deal with the whole broad question of armament reduction. This body which became one of the best-known instruments of the League of Nations, was called the Temporary Mixed Commission, "temporary" because it was not one of the permanent organizations of the League, "mixed" because of its mixed membership. During the next three years, from March, 1921, this body played the major part in all discussions on and plans for the reduction of armaments, and during most of that period it was largely influenced by the untiring efforts of Lord Robert Cecil (later Viscount Cecil).

While the League was thus getting its organization in shape to deal with the problem of armament, Secretary Charles Evans Hughes called the Washington Naval Conference in the winter of 1921–22 and at once took the bold step of proposing an actual cutting down on capital ships to a ratio of 5:5:3 for the United States, Great Britain and Japan, the three great naval powers. The effect of this dramatic act was prodigious. It looked as though a measuring rod had been found by which capital ships, the chief element in sea power, could be calculated so that a certain amount of tonnage should be assigned to the nations possessing them. The formula 5:5:3 became a popular slogan, not only in the United States, and that section of the peace movement which had been emphasizing the importance of disarmament summarized its confident hope of future developments in the phrase, "The way to peace is by disarmament and the way to disarm is to disarm." In all of this the political reality that underlay the Washington Conference was lost sight of; this was the denunciation of the alliance between Great Britain and Japan, an act due to the influence of Canada. No mathematical formula could have worked out with the easy balance of that of the Washington Conference if British and Japanese armaments had remained allied. The public, however, paid little attention to the underlying fact of politics and for the time being regarded the Washington disarmament method as the one and only way to secure results.

The effect of this interlude in the history of disarmament, for that is what it turned out to be, was felt immediately in Europe and at Geneva. There the effort was made by Lord Esher to apply the arithmetical ratio to the standing armies of Europe, taking as a unit in manpower 30,000 men for the military and air forces, and thus to find a parallel to what had been done in naval parity. But it soon became clear that this method of comparison by arithmetical ratios was utterly unreal. The realistic French and others as well pointed out that any such scheme as this offered no solution to nations differing in geographic position, moral or economic capacities. Nations with open frontiers had a greater need for artificial defense than those with mountains, rivers or oceans separating them from their neighbors. Moreover, the warfare of the future was bound to be more and more conditioned by the advances of science. It was already evident that the chemists would replace the weapons of the past by those capable of mass destruction for which the old ratios of ship tonnage and manpower were practically meaningless.

In the structure of the League of Nations these major issues of long-term plans and policies belonged clearly within the province of the Assembly rather than of the Council, a theory repeated in the Charter of the United Nations. It was, therefore, inevitable that in the Third Assembly of 1922 the old question of armament reduction should come up for review. The result was a restatement of the problem along lines utterly at variance with those followed by the extreme advocates of disarmament in America. The Assembly turned the problem end for end and stated in the famous Resolution XIV[1] that the prior question was that of national security and that no scheme for the reduction of armaments could succeed unless the countries concerned received in exchange a satisfactory guarantee of their safety. The Resolution went on then to state that the only guarantee that could be effective would be a well-organized system of collective security.

The importance of Resolution XIV cannot be minimized. In it the League of Nations definitely turned away from the over-simplified theory of the Washington Conference and accepted the French thesis that no government can imperil the safety of its country by lessening its armaments without regard to other means for insuring its safety. This was getting back to realities. It was also a recognition of the intricacy and difficulty of the problem itself.

With reference to this last point, however, it should be said that in 1922 there was still real optimism that collective security as the alternative to armaments was not too difficult a problem for the League to work out in detail. This was the task of the Temporary Mixed Commission, and throughout 1922 and the early months of 1923 Lord Robert Cecil and his colleagues worked tirelessly on the drafting of a "Treaty of Mutual Assistance," which was to be submitted to the Assembly of the League as a basis for the reduction of armaments.

[1]For the text of Resolution XIV, see Appendix, pp. 111–112.

4. THE TREATY OF MUTUAL ASSISTANCE
AND THE AMERICAN PLAN

THE OPENING WORDS of this Draft Treaty showed that its framers were no longer thinking within the purely technical field of armaments but were attacking militarism itself. For it began with the declaration that aggressive war is a crime. It could be argued that this was implied in the Covenant of the League but nowhere had it been stated in the text of a treaty. Starting from this premise, the Draft Treaty proposed a more definite program for the sanctions of the League against an aggressor, and on the basis of that stronger and more definite assurance of mutual assistance called for programs of progressive reduction of armaments.

This, however, was going too fast and far for the military experts on the Permanent Commission. The French General Staff and the British Admiralty were equally opposed to relying upon provision for collective security as an adequate basis for any major measures of armament reduction. This was the summer of 1923. It was evident that if the Draft Treaty of Mutual Assistance were to come up for final disposal at the Assembly of 1923 the result would be most disappointing. Fortunately, that issue was not directly joined and the work of the Temporary Mixed Commission continued throughout the following year.

The situation was a serious one for the League because it began to look as though it would not be able to deal with the most important general problem on its program. In view of the importance which public opinion still attached to the question of armament reduction, the League's failure in this field would have been little short of disastrous. Yet the Draft Treaty rested on the uncertain basis of a declaration that aggressive war is a crime, without, however, defining aggression.

It was at this point that an unofficial American Committee undertook to study the problem, and in order to make its suggestions definite and realistic, drew them up in the form of a Draft Treaty. This followed for the most part the lines of the Treaty of Mutual Assistance but included as well a test of aggression. This was stated in the simplest possible terms as the resort to war while refusing the pacific means of settlement which the nation in question had previously accepted in obligations under the League or in this treaty. In view of the fact that the United States was not a member of the League, the test of aggression was stated in terms which would apply to it and, therefore, the Permanent Court of International Justice was indicated as the body which should have jurisdiction over any alleged act of aggression, and refusal to submit to it while pursuing the alleged aggression would bring upon the recalcitrant nation a new kind of sanction. This was the outlawry of the aggressor by denying it the protection of either international law, national law or treaty.

It was obvious that this form of sanction was much less sweeping than those under Article 16 of the League Covenant. But it was one thing for the Covenant to be strong in the letter of the law and a wholly different thing for the members of the League of Nations to live up to the Covenant. Then, there was the further point that the refusal of the United States to join the League had been largely due to its reluctance to accept the obligation of the sanctions as set forth in the Covenant, for the very reason that it would have to participate in the enforcement of "collective security." It was mainly for this last reason that the unofficial Draft Treaty proposed a commitment which did not involve actual policing, but deprived the aggressor of the protection of law.

The text of this section of the Draft Treaty read as follows:

ARTICLE 8.—In the event of any H. C. P. [High Contracting Party] having been adjudged an aggressor pursuant to this Treaty, all commercial, trade, financial and property interests of the aggressor and of its nationals shall cease to be entitled, either in the territories of the other Signatories or on the high seas, to any privileges, protection, rights or immunities accorded by either international law, national law or treaty.

Any H. C. P. may in such case take such other steps toward the severance of trade, financial, commercial and personal intercourse with the aggressor and its nationals as it may deem proper and the H. C. P. may also consult together in this regard.

The period during which any such economic sanction may be continued shall be fixed at any time by the Court at the request of any Signatory.

In the matter of measures of force to be taken, each Signatory shall consult its own interests and obligations.

ARTICLE 9.—If any H. C. P. shall be adjudged an aggressor by the Permanent Court of International Justice, such Power shall be liable for all costs to all other H. C. P. resulting from its aggression.

It is easy to understand the opposition which this apparent effort to weaken the sanctions of the Covenant would meet in Geneva. And yet, the proponents of the proposal felt that it was by no means so weak as its opponents thought it to be. The fact that an aggressor nation would automatically lose the security of its property and that of its nationals in dealing with other countries introduced a new principle of international law. If such a provision were adopted in a universal treaty it would certainly have a very great effect upon business interests. No trader could be sure that his ships would receive entry into the ports of another Signatory or that his investments in their keeping would not be immediately attached. In a world built upon the basis of credit, the result might very well be disastrous for the aggressor. This, at least, was the argument raised against the proposal by conservative international lawyers who felt that it was a step backward from the tendency of international law toward safeguarding private property rights in the midst of war. The answer to that was that the laws of war were undergoing a complete revolution in the effort to stop it altogether. The theory of international law that war could be made more and more humane had been completely disproved by the total war of modern science as experienced in the first World War. Therefore, the sanctions against it should be the strongest that it was possible to impose. The question of the sanction really narrowed down to this: What was the strongest measure against war which nations would be ready to apply in collective security? The American Plan, while not in any way denying the validity of the military and economic sanctions of the Covenant as set forth in Article 16, took a long step in the same direction in strengthening and extending the economic sanctions. The history of the next few years went to show that even this was going farther than the Great Powers within the League of Nations were willing to go. In the League Assembly of 1924, however, the argument for strong military sanctions prevailed and the result was the Protocol of Geneva.

The Draft Treaty also covered the problem of international inspection of armaments. This was in Part III (Articles 18–22) which bore the innocuous title "International Information" but provided for inspection by a Commission of the League of Nations in any country on the state of armaments; and the signatories were to "give all necessary facilities to the said Commission in the performance of its duties" (Article 21). This Article did not occur in the League's Draft Treaty of Mutual Assistance (Lord Cecil's) which left it to each signatory "to cooperate with the League and to supply information."

It was this body which General Tasker Howard Bliss and General James Guthrie Harbord, members of the American Committee, regarded as the real instrument of disarmament. Also, Lord Haldane, in a letter commenting upon the Treaty, stated that he regarded this as its chief contribution and that in his opinion it had greatly improved on any previous formulation. It is a long way, however, from this pioneering suggestion to anything like practical fulfillment.

5. THE PROTOCOL OF GENEVA

THE WHOLE ISSUE was threshed out at the League Assembly of 1924, and the result was agreement upon what became known as the Protocol of Geneva.[1] The only contribution of the American Draft Treaty which was actually taken up and adopted in the Protocol was the definition of aggression. But without that, no agreement whatever would have been reached. Unless a distinction could be drawn between the illegitimate resort to force by a State, and its admitted right of self-defence which might also assume the proportions of war, the effort to eliminate war as an instrument of national policy was nothing more than a futile gesture. The Protocol improved upon the American draft by making the test of aggression the refusal to resort to the appropriate judicial, arbitral or mediatory organs for procuring peaceful settlement of disputes. M. Édouard Herriot summed up the whole issue in a single sentence: "The aggressor is the one who refuses arbitration." It was soon seen, however, that the word "arbitration" was used in the broadest possible sense and that it applied to any procedure which settled a dispute peaceably. Article 10 of the Protocol stated that "every State that resorts to war in violation of the undertakings contained in the Covenant or in the present Protocol is an aggressor." As the Protocol presented an ironclad rule against resort to war by any State on its own account, no matter what the provocation, but turned over to the collective action of the League all redress of grievances or settlements of disputes, the "hole in the Covenant" had apparently at last been plugged. The right of warfare was henceforth denied to

[1]For text see Appendix, pp. 113–124.

24

sovereign States, and that attribute of sovereignty was taken over by the collective action of the League.

This revolutionary step was not taken without debate. It was pointed out, especially by the Swedish delegate, Dr. Unden, that the test of aggression as set forth in Article 10 of the Protocol involved questions of fact which called for investigation in a period of crisis when time might be lacking for it, and that all that one could say was that the test established "the presumption of aggression." On the other hand, the point was made that to establish the presumption of aggression by such a test as that established in the Protocol would in itself have a strong preventive tendency in the direction of policies of state, and that the prevention of war itself lay more in this field of policy than in complete reliance upon the fulfillment of technical legal obligations. The Protocol, however, added an important test in the proposal for demilitarized zones such as those already established in the Treaty of Versailles. The violation of such a zone would be the clearest possible sign of an aggressive act. More important still was the provision that in the event of hostilities having broken out, the Council could impose an armistice and that any State violating that armistice should be deemed an aggressor.

The Protocol of Geneva was the high-water mark of the history of the League of Nations as an organization for the maintenance of enduring peace. It was the longest step ever made by the League or any other international body to "outlaw war," to use the phrase then current in the United States. It had the support of all the Continental European nations, Members of the League, and even in Germany there was a large movement of public opinion in its favor. Unfortunately, however, both for the League and for the peace of the world, in the autumn of 1924 a Conservative government came into power in Great Britain, utterly out of sympathy with the basic principle of the Protocol, that which made membership in the League an ironclad obligation to join the prevention of war anywhere in the world.

In justification of the action of the British Conservatives, it must be remembered that this commitment to an "indefinite obligation" to maintain peace anywhere was contrary to established British policy and, indeed, to the established policy of all other nations, and more especially the United States. It was argued by supporters of the League that the Covenant itself involved the same kind of "indefinite obligation" on the part of League Members, but the Protocol brought home this "interference with sovereignty" in a way in which it had never been realized before. In any case, the British Government shied off from the Protocol and the League was apparently left weaker than ever before, because it was evident that in reality the British Government could not be counted upon to carry out the equally general obligations of the Covenant.

The failure of the Protocol involved as well a further obstacle in the pathway of disarmament. The Protocol had provided that a disarmament conference should be summoned for June 15, 1925, and linked together the two questions of security and disarmament by the provision that the Protocol itself would not come into force until the plan for the reduction of armaments had been adopted by the Disarmament Conference (Article 21).

The Assembly of 1925, therefore, made a new start at the problem of disarmament by setting up the Preparatory Committee for the Disarmament Conference.

6. THE TREATIES OF LOCARNO

FORTUNATELY FOR THE British Government, Germany came to the rescue. Articles began to appear in the Cologne Gazette suggesting that there might be a limited regional guarantee of peace between France and Germany on the condition that both nations would be willing to sign a nonaggression treaty under the guarantee of two neutral nations, Great Britain and Italy. This suggestion was eagerly taken up by Sir Austen Chamberlain, British Foreign Minister, and led to the treaties of Locarno[1] in the late summer of 1925. In these, the British Government undertook the limited regional guarantee against the aggressor which it had refused to take in the general terms of the Protocol. For example, on the Western front it would guarantee peace as against either France or Germany if either of those nations went to war refusing "to submit a dispute to peaceful settlement or to comply with an arbitral or judicial decision or submit to the action of the Council of the League of Nations." In Article 5 which contains this guarantee the signatories of Locarno really accepted the test of aggression of the Protocol, although it must be admitted that they did not seem to have realized at the time that they were doing so.

The world was now to learn whether regional and limited guarantees of peace such as the Locarno treaties were more to be relied upon than the general and universal obligations of the Covenant or the Protocol. For a few years Europe lived peacefully under the Locarno regime; and acting under its sense of security, Britain proceeded to lessen its armaments and grant some naval armament

[1] For text see 54 League of Nations Treaty Series, p. 289.

concessions to Germany, while France began to limit its armaments to such defensive plans as those which matured in the Maginot Line. It was not long, however, until Hitler seized power and, proceeding both secretly and openly to violate the armament restrictions of the treaty of Versailles, prepared to test the validity of the Locarno policy. The first step, after rearmament, was the invasion of the Rhineland. The regional guarantee was tested first of all when Britain found ample excuse for the German action in the recovery of German territory. Lacking support by the British, the French also remained inactive. The next step around the frontier was Hitler's invasion of Austria, and although this was a much more serious violation of Locarno, the arguments in its favor were sufficiently familiar and nothing was done. Next came Czechoslovakia and at Munich it was at last evident that regional security was a fraudulent formula for the peace of Europe. Finally, after the betrayal of Czechoslovakia when the whole strategic position was absolutely in Germany's favor, Britain and France went to war on the last violation of the regional guarantees, that of Poland. Yet, in order to keep this history straight, it should be noted here that the British Government definitely stated as it went to war in September, 1939, that it was not just to save Poland but to maintain the good faith of nations and the observation of international treaties. Too late the British Government and people found that the regional guarantees which had been relied upon as a substitute for the Protocol and as an implementation of the Covenant offered no real guarantee against aggression. The Protocol of Geneva which had implemented Article 11 of the Covenant and had provided against any and all violations of it had been the one last bulwark of European peace.

Turning to the texts of the Locarno Treaties, it will be recalled that in addition to the Treaty of Mutual Guarantee between Germany, Belgium, France, Great Britain and Italy, there were also four Arbitration Conventions signed by Germany and its neighbors, Belgium, France, Poland and Czechoslovakia. These Conventions, as we shall see, are of special interest in connection with this study.

The Treaty itself guaranteed the maintenance of the territorial *status quo* of the Treaty of Versailles and an undertaking to settle all disputes by peaceful means by either judicial decision or by the procedure of conciliation, with a further provision that in the last resort the question should go before the Council of the League under Article 15 of the Covenant. Article 4 of the Treaty provided that "an unprovoked act of aggression such as crossing the frontier . . . or the assembly of armed forces in the demilitarized zone, would call for immediate joint action by the guarantors of the peace." Article 5 went on to define aggression in the broader sense as the refusal to submit a dispute to peaceful settlement or to comply with an arbitral or judicial decision or to use the instrumentality offered by the League of Nations itself. This was the spelling out of the definition of aggression of the Protocol of Geneva, referred to above.

The Arbitration Conventions referred juridical questions either to an arbitral tribunal or to the Permanent Court of International Justice. But Article 2 provided that

before any resort is made to arbitral procedure or to procedure before the Permanent Court of International Justice, the dispute may, by agreement between the parties, be submitted, with a view to amicable settlement, to a permanent international commission styled the Permanent Conciliation Commission, constituted in accordance with the present Convention.

Article 4 provided for the constitution of this Permanent Conciliation Commission. It was to be composed of five members, one from Germany and the other from the neighboring State in question, chosen "from among their respective nationals" and by common agreement, three other commissioners of different nationalities. The term of the commissioners was for three years and their mandate renewable.

The function of the Permanent Conciliation Commission was set forth in Article 8:

The task of the Permanent Conciliation Commission shall be to elucidate questions in dispute, to collect with that object all necessary information by means of enquiry or otherwise, and to endeavour to bring the parties to an agreement. It may, after the case has been examined, inform the parties of the terms of settlement which seem suitable to it, and lay down a period within which they are to make their decision.

At the close of its labours the commission shall draw up a report stating, as the case may be, either that the parties have come to an agreement and, if need arises, the terms of the agreement, or that it has been impossible to effect a settlement.

The labours of the commission must, unless the parties otherwise agree, be terminated within six months from the day on which the commission shall have been notified of the dispute.

The Convention went on to provide that the Conciliation Commission should not meet in public "except when a decision to that effect has been taken by the Commission with the consent of the parties"(Article 11). It could lay down its own procedure and "unless otherwise provided in the present Convention," its decisions should be taken by majority (Article 13).

These were the chief points in the final Protocol of the Locarno Conference. It will be seen that they were copied and applied in the subsequent proposals of the League and of the Disarmament Conference.

Finally, it should be recalled that as a result of the Locarno Agreements it was agreed that Germany should enter the League of Nations. This took place in 1926.

7. PROPOSALS TO ORGANIZE PEACE

THE NEXT FEW YEARS in European history were what was termed the era of Locarno, a period in which it looked as if, alongside the universal League, something resembling the old concert of Europe had come to life again, thus giving a double guarantee of peace. Although the League had suffered a blow in the failure of the Protocol of Geneva of 1924, its brilliant success in stopping the Greco-Bulgar threat of war in the autumn of 1925 raised its prestige once more to a high level. It was under these conditions that work was finally begun upon the actual preparation for a disarmament Conference. Already in December, 1924, the Council had set up a Preparatory Committee for the Disarmament Conference, to take over whatever results were left from the long effort of the Temporary Mixed Commission. The plan now, however, was to call a Disarmament Conference and have it draw up its own plans and deal directly with the governments. But while the League to some extent stepped aside in this procedure, the preparatory work for the Conference was carried on in close connection with the instrumentalities of the League.

Public opinion everywhere regarded the work of the Disarmament Conference as a function of the League. Technically, however, it was an autonomous body, and as such its history has been treated separately in the following section. The Preparatory Committee, however, did not limit itself to the problem of the limitation of armaments but, in full accord with the spirit of Resolution XIV of the Assembly of 1922, concentrated upon the prior issue of national security. This effort of the League to create preparatory instruments for dealing with international disputes has never been properly appreciated because the tests of these instruments by the aggressor powers came before there was time to mobilize sufficient political support for them, or even a full understanding of their import. The guarantee of security does not lie in the technical excellence or perfection of a document, but in the will to observe its obligations. If international commitments are to be respected, nations must have an alert consciousness of their binding quality and of the consequences of violation. Unfortunately, the era of the League of Nations was too short to create that fundamental change in international political relations which is involved in shifting the basis of policy from power politics to collective action. Had the statesmanship of the 1920's been of the relatively cautious type of the nineteenth century instead of having to face the violently revolutionary imperialism of the Axis Powers, these instruments of pacification and disarmament might have had a better fate.

This work of the Preparatory Committee to strengthen the guarantee of security by provision for the peaceful settlement of disputes resulted in two draft treaties, the General Act of 1928[1] and the Draft Treaty to Develop the Means for Preventing War of September, 1931.[2] Both of these documents, now almost entirely forgotten, are of interest to any serious student of the immensely difficult problems involved in the erection of a structure of enduring peace.

The date of the General Act, September, 1928, is itself significant. The previous month had witnessed the conclusion of the long drawn out negotiations between M. Briand and Secretary of State Frank B. Kellogg, which resulted in the Pact of Paris, signed in a solemn ceremony at the Quai d'Orsay in August, 1928. While none of the events connected with this chapter of the history of the Peace movement took place in Geneva, it was not without influence within the circle of the League of Nations. The proposal originated out of a letter of M. Briand of April 26, 1927, on the occasion of the tenth anniversary of the entrance of the United States into the World War, in which M. Briand proposed "to subscribe publicly with the United

[1] For text see Appendix, pp. 125–138.
[2] For text see Appendix, pp. 139–143.

States to any mutual engagement tending to outlaw war, to use an American expression, as between these two countries." The words "any engagement," showed that M. Briand was thinking in very general terms, but the next sentence of his letter indicated that the proposal did not lie outside of or in any way athwart the purposes of the League of Nations. "The renunciation of war as an instrument of national policy is a conception already familiar to the signatories of the Covenant of the League of Nations and of the Treaties of Locarno." Mr. Kellogg negotiated along a wholly different line in keeping his treaty free from any attempt to impose a sanction upon the violator and in refusing to limit the obligation to wars of aggression. History was to show that the American amendment to M. Briand's proposal made the document both meaningless and futile. In his speech at the ceremony of the signature, M. Briand indicated the nature of the unfinished task. "Peace has been proclaimed. That is well. That is much. But peace has yet to be organized. For settlement by force we must substitute settlement by law. That must be the work of tomorrow."

This "work of tomorrow" had already been begun in September, 1927, when the League Assembly directed the Preparatory Commission for the Disarmament Conference (set up the previous year), to appoint a subcommittee on Arbitration and Security. The Assembly Resolution had a definitely practical aim, for it requested the new committee "to consider . . . the measures capable of giving all States the guarantees of arbitration and security necessary to enable them to fix the level of their armaments at the lowest possible figures in an international disarmament agreement."

Its program was to include action by the League itself "to promote, generalize and co-ordinate special collective agreements on aggression and security" and to prepare the necessary machinery in that connection. It also was to suggest agreements among the Members themselves in support of Council recommendations and in the event of a crisis.

At the first meeting of the Committee on Arbitration and Security, which took place on December 1 and 2, 1927, three *Rapporteurs* were appointed to study the various aspects of the Committee's

work. Arbitration was assigned to M. Holsti (Finland); Security
to M. Politis (Greece); and Articles of the Covenant, 10, 11 and 16
to M. Rutgers (Netherlands). The Committee, having been organized with M. Eduard Benes as Chairman, circularized the States
members of the League, asking for their suggestions on the problems
before it. The Norwegians proposed a hard and fast commitment
that "the contracting parties would undertake to accept as binding
the conclusions of the Council's report if it were accepted unanimously, the votes of the representatives of the parties not being
counted in reckoning this unanimity." A decision taken by the
Council under Article 15, paragraph 8, of the Covenant should also
be binding. The British memorandum was definitely opposed to
this extension of the powers of the Council in what amounted to a
compulsory arbitration. Sensitive to dominion opposition to compulsory jurisdiction and uncertain of United States support at a
critical moment, the British Government repeated once more its
conviction that international politics, like domestic politics, were
primarily a matter of public opinion and that provision for police
action in international affairs could not be relied upon, no matter
what the commitment, if the nations concerned were not convinced
at the time of the necessity of the action. "Arbitration duties have
no sanction behind them but the force of public opinion in the
world at large. Any attempt to provide sanctions of force would
involve a burden which no state could accept unless it felt that its
vital interests were involved in a particular dispute."

The British reluctance to accept compulsory arbitration by extending the powers of the Council of the League was in line with the
trend of American public opinion which at that time was being
carried to the limit by the wing of the peace movement which was
led by Senator William E. Borah and which for the time being
dominated the State Department. While even the Conservative
British Government had no thought of going so far as Borah's proposal to rely wholly upon public opinion as the sanction against
aggression, it pointed out that the result of an effort to establish
compulsory arbitration would be an elaborate system of reservations.
Conciliation procedure instead of arbitration was advocated for

political disputes and the regional system of Locarno for security pacts as between nations.

The German Government agreed with the British that guarantees were not necessary for the enforcement of arbitration and that non-justiciable disputes could best be dealt with by conciliation. It insisted that the prevention of the outbreak of war was the point of departure instead of the provision of military sanctions against a breach already committed. The latter method would be "like trying to build a house from the roof downward. War cannot be prevented by preparing for a war against war, but only by removing its causes." At this point the German Government differed from the British in insisting that the organization of peace should be universal and not merely regional.

With this memorandum serving as a basis, three reports were drawn up; the report on arbitration by M. Holsti traced the growing tendency to abandon reservations and restrictions on arbitration and conciliation treaties. It suggested that obligatory arbitration be limited to justiciable disputes and that conciliation procedure be followed in other cases.

M. Politis' report on security is especially interesting because it shows the sobering effect of the failure of the Protocol of Geneva upon one of its chief architects. He was now ready to give up the ironclad provisions for the maintenance of peace through a strong system of sanctions, which had been the central idea of the guarantee of the Protocol. Conforming to the influence of the Locarno era, he was now ready to admit that "the conclusion of a general treaty binding on all States Members of the League . . . must be excluded, if it were to contain a rigid obligation for enforcement against an aggressor." He, therefore, proposed that the Committee draft a comprehensive series of treaties against aggressive war, for the pacific settlement of disputes, and for a system of mutual assistance. The regional agreements should be linked together in harmony with the Covenant.

M. Rutgers' report is of special interest. Although it is in the shape of a commentary on Articles 10, 11 and 16 of the Covenant, in reality it covers a wide range of diplomatic history in connection with these major articles of the Covenant. After a careful analysis of the operations called for under these articles in the prevention and suppression of aggressive war, it ends with a series of thoughtful and suggestive conclusions, of which the following are the more pertinent for the purposes of this study.

It does not seem advisable to draw up a rigid and complete code of procedure for the League in times of emergency, and the present memorandum and its conclusions propose neither to extend nor to curtail the rights and duties of the Members of the League.

It is both feasible and desirable, however, to give some indication of the possibilities offered by the different articles of the Covenant and the way in which they may be applied, without expressing any opinion as to the particular methods which the infinite variety of possible cases may in practice require.

The task of the League of Nations is to maintain peace; to fulfil the task it must, above all *prevent* war. The application of repressive measures, which cannot but have serious consequences, will only take place in extreme cases in which the preventive measures have unfortunately failed in their object.

A hard-and-fast definition of the expression "aggression" (Article 10), and "resort to war" (Article 16) would not be free from danger, since it might oblige the Council and the Members of the League to pronounce on a breach of the Covenant and apply sanctions at a time when it would still be preferable to refrain for the moment from measures of coercion. There would also be the risk that criteria might be taken which, in unforeseen circumstances, might lead to a State which was not in reality responsible for hostilities being described as an aggressor.

The preparation of the military sanctions provided for in Article 16 does not seem likely to promote mutual confidence between the States Members of the League of Nations unless at the same time various forms of pacific procedure suitable for the settlement of all international disputes are organised, and unless there is also a general agreement on the reduction and limitation of armaments.

It would be well that, in the event of resort to war, the Council should declare whether a breach of the Covenant has or has not taken place, and should state which of the two parties to the dispute has broken the Covenant.

In determining the aggressor the Council will find, among other factors helping it to form a judgment, a valuable indication in the extent to which and the manner in which the parties to the dispute have promoted the action previously taken by the Council in application of the articles of the Covenant, and especially of Article 11, to maintain peace.

Apart from the recommendations provided for in paragraph 2 of Article 16 concerning participation in military sanctions, it would be desirable for the Council in some cases to make recommendations to the Members regarding the application of the measures of economic pressure mentioned in the first paragraph of Article 16. In this eventuality, the Council could consult economic and financial experts in the countries specially concerned.

The study of the question of the financial assistance to be given to a State victim of an aggression should be pursued both from the technical and the political points of view. In carrying out this study, the possibility of providing assistance, even before Article 16 is applied, should be examined.

The Committee on Arbitration and Security had a second meeting from February 20 to March 7, 1928, which showed that the alignments of the delegations into two camps continued without much change. France and her allies still looked to the Geneva Protocol, while Great Britain, Italy and Japan opposed any such kind of Convention. Out of the discussions came three texts of multilateral conventions, the provisions of which were incorporated in the General Act for the Pacific Settlement of Disputes which was finally adopted by the Assembly in September, 1928.

The first two of these draft conventions dealt with the compulsory procedure of either arbitral or judicial disputes. Although drafted with great experience and skill, neither of these proposed conventions are of practical interest because of the necessary limitation upon compulsory jurisdiction in cases where the definite verdict or settlement would be insisted upon. On the other hand the Convention for conciliation (Convention C) is of continuing and vital interest because it aims primarily to prevent disputes from reaching the stage of overt acts or even of rigidly conceived questions of right, and deals with the matters under dispute on political rather than legal terms. It was recognized that the mere provision for the setting up of a conciliatory commission was not enough and that conciliation was but the open door to definite settlements. It put the main emphasis, however, upon the securing of a common approach to the matter of the dispute so that the need for compulsory measures would be substantially lessened and perhaps completely eliminated.

The idea of the procedure of conciliation was to provide an incentive for agreement rather than to threaten a punishment for disagreement. The latter alternative, however, would still remain under the Covenant of the League, if there were acts of aggression arising from the dispute.

The Committee on Arbitration and Security had a third meeting on June 27 to July 4, 1928, at which the German Government made an interesting proposal to make the recommendations of the Council for preventing war binding upon States Members of the League. The proposal was that there should be another Protocol of Geneva in which the signatories would bind themselves in advance to accept the Council's recommendations whenever there was a dispute that actually threatened war. This proposal failed of adoption because of the opposition of the English and Italian delegates, while the French and their allies argued that such a provision did not really contribute to security so long as there was no obligation to follow through with the sanctions.

By the time the Ninth Assembly of the League met in September, 1928, the Committee had proposed ten draft treaties. The Assembly speedily reduced this body of proposals to one General Act of four chapters based upon the three multilateral conventions. It was the final word of the League of Nations in the erection of a correlative system of safeguards of peace alongside the Covenant itself. Profiting from the lessons of recent history, it did not attempt to follow the model of the Protocol of Geneva in the effort to "outlaw war." It dealt only with the strengthening of the alternatives for war in providing at the very least a program for the nations to follow in the arrangements which they could make between themselves for the pacific settlement of disputes. Instead of attempting to force the acceptance of its provisions upon all nations without due regard to their conditions, it attempted a whole series of reservations and even allowed a signatory to extend its reservations by a simple declaration, on the principle that there would be more likelihood that the Act would actually be invoked in a dispute if there were a freedom of choice as to the exact extent to which it would be applied.

The Assembly approved the Joint Act by unanimous vote, and by 1936, twenty-three States had adhered to it.

8. THE TREATY TO DEVELOP THE MEANS
FOR PREVENTING WAR

THE FAR-REACHING ACTIVITIES of the Committee on Arbitration and Security of the Preparatory Commission on Disarmament did not stop with the General Act for the Pacific Settlement of Disputes which we have just been reviewing. Early in the course of its discussions the German delegate, Dr. von Simson, came forward with a proposal to explore more fully the prevention of war under Article 11 of the Covenant rather than the sanctions under Article 16. The German proposals are of special interest, not only on account of their realistic character, but also of the source from which they came. Aggression, said Dr. von Simson, will not be stopped by threatening the aggressor with future sanctions but by placing impediments in the path of policies of aggression while insisting upon the use of conciliation as the alternative for the resort to force. The problem lies in dealing with disputes of a political character, for justiciable matters have already been provided for in both court and arbitral procedures.

The procedure of conciliation unfortunately takes time and, therefore, it is extremely important to prevent any steps being taken during the preliminary period of organization of conciliation, which might have a prejudicial effect on the solution of the dispute.

Going back to the procedure of the Protocol and of the Locarno Treaties, the German delegate proposed that during the time of crisis the States undertake to respect the military *status quo* or if necessary to restore a disturbed *status quo* on the request of the Council. "In this connection we might have recourse to the procedure of an injunction." It is already late to apply conciliation when events are following the deadly time table of the general staffs. "It is extremely important not only to prevent States from prejudicing the final solution but also to prevent them from embarking upon military preparations, which often have more influence on events than the pacific endeavor of responsible statesmen."

The effort to stop hostilities in preparation would naturally be carried over into the period in which fighting had already begun. Therefore, the Council should be invested with the right to recommend an armistice. The point of view of the German Government was that the provisions of the Protocol for defining the aggressor were too closely connected with the idea of preventing war by collective sanction and not enough for securing the continuance of peace for the purpose of setting up an adequate substitute for war. The emphasis should be changed from punishment to prevention. Even the idea of compulsory armistice in the Locarno Agreements is not a good model for use elsewhere because there is lacking any general treaty on conciliation pure and simple.

Politis readily accepted the German delegate's statement that the essential aim is "not to suppress the war which has already broken out but to establish measures which may prevent it from arising," but he reminded the Committee that with a young and untried organization as the League of Nations "the two ideas cannot be separated." Lord Cushenden, from the standpoint of the Conservative British Government of the day, took a definitely negative stand against the German proposal for a preliminary armistice between contesting nations. "Is it likely," he said, "that the aggressor state, having made up its mind to incur all the odium and all the danger of acting in a way which will inevitably bring down upon it the disapproval of the League of Nations . . . will at the last moment withdraw its troops which have gone over a frontier or stay its hand at the moment of aggression when it perhaps has an advantage over somebody else which it may never have at a later stage?"

Dr. von Simson replied that the ambiguities in his plan would be ironed out under the disarmament proposals and for purposes of clarity read a purely hypothetical series of propositions at the meeting of the Committee on February 22, 1928. This document was almost in the nature of a draft for a treaty and is worth quoting on that account, but it should be clearly understood that the text was never intended for more than a basis for discussion.

I

In case of a dispute being submitted to the Council, the States might undertake in advance to accept and execute provisional recommendations of the Council for the purpose of preventing any aggravation or extension of the dispute and impeding any measures which might be taken by the parties and which might have an unfavorable effect on the execution of the settlement to be proposed by the Council.

II

In case of a threat of war, the States might undertake in advance to accept and to execute the recommendations of the Council to the effect of maintaining or re-establishing the military *status quo* normally existing in time of peace.

III

In the case of hostilities of any kind having broken out without, in the Council's opinion, all possibilities of a pacific settlement having been exhausted, the States might undertake in advance to accept, on the Council's proposal, an armistice on land and sea and in the air, including especially the obligation, for the two parties in dispute, to withdraw any forces which might have penetrated into foreign territory and to respect the sovereignty of the other State.

IV

The question should be considered whether the above obligations should be undertaken only in case of unanimous vote of the Council (the votes of the parties in dispute not being counted), or whether a majority, simple or qualified, should suffice in the matter. Furthermore, it should be considered in what form the obligations would have to be drawn up in order to bring them into conformity with the Covenant.

V

These obligations might constitute the subject of an agreement or of a protocol which would be open for signature by all States Members and non-Members of the League of Nations, and which might come into force separately for the several continents in a way similar to that provided for in the draft Treaty of Mutual Assistance of 1923.

On the basis of these suggestions, M. Rolin-Jacquemyns, the Belgian delegate, presented to the Committee on Arbitration and Security at its summer session, a model treaty which was adopted by the Assembly on September 22, 1928, after discussion in the Third Committee. The purpose of this draft was to furnish guidance in the conduct of direct negotiations between States for the drafting of multilateral treaties along the lines of this model. The possibility of using this model for bilateral treaties as well was not excluded. It was felt that no one general convention would be applicable to all the varying details of the conditions in the relation of the different States, but the model treaty had at least the merit of affirming that the League should work more definitely in the realm of prevention.

At the Tenth Assembly in 1929, Lord Cecil proposed that the question should be taken up again by its Third Commission and the result was that the Committee on Arbitration and Security was asked to draft a General Convention along the lines of the model treaty. In May, 1930, the Committee reported progress. But it was held back by the insistence of Poland and the Little Entente countries that the Council should have precise powers and that ambiguity would lessen not only the sense of security but its reality. Going back to the principles of the Protocol, they asked that the Council should be given the definite authority to order the retreat of armed forces which had invaded a country or a demilitarized zone. The delegation of Germany joined with the English at this point to take sides against the French-Little Entente reliance upon the assertion of a stronger sanction, and indicated their fears that for the Council to enumerate definite and positive measures might really lessen its general powers under Article 11.

Finally, on January 23, 1930, acting on the invitation of the Eleventh Assembly, the Council appointed a special committee to draft a text that would take due account of all these variant trends. This committee, under the Chairmanship of M. Politis, in May, 1931, elaborated a convention which, after some slight modification by the Third Commission of the Twelfth Assembly, was finally adopted, on motion of M. Salvador de Madariaga, in September, 1931, and was open to signature of the States.

This General Convention had one very important principle. The parties engaged to accept and put into execution the decisions which the Council might take in case of an acute dispute between the nations. In this way the weakness of the action of the Council under Article 11, which had already been brought out in an earlier report, that the Council's decisions under Article 11 were not juridically binding, was overcome. The new convention was prepared to be applicable to any foreseeable case and obligatory in any and every conflict that might arise.

By a tragic coincidence this was the very time when the Japanese militarists took what proved to be the first definite step on the pathway to World War II, in the local attack upon the Chinese at the station of Mukden in Manchuria.

II

A Comprehensive Survey of Security Disputes before the Council

THE JUDGMENT of history on the League of Nations will rest largely on such evidence as is here assembled concerning the major political issues in the field of security which came before the Council for settlement; yet, strange as it may seem, this is the first time the whole evidence has been surveyed. The only comprehensive study previously made of this material was the manual, still valuable, of Conwell Evans, *The League Council in Action;* but it was published in 1929, before the final stage of League history.

The study which follows is limited to a factual survey, with no editorial comment in each case, but a thoughtful examination of the record reveals at least two essential principles which are still, and will always be, of complete validity.

The first is that the political settlement of disputes, in contrast with juristic measures, calls first for efforts to secure an attitude of compromise on the part of the contestants, a willingness, if need be, to back away from hard and fast decisions of policy. This generally involves the weighing of the point at issue with other elements in the relationships of the two parties. In some cases this is merely a recognition of the fact that a peaceful settlement is better than enforcing the whole of a claim against an opponent by violent measures which would cause more damage than could possibly be compensated for, or create a future situation disadvantageous to the victor because of the interests of other nations. In short, the procedure of conciliation, which was the major method of the Council, could be successful when the alternative consequences—quite apart from any sanctions of the League—were of a kind to be avoided by any responsible government.

This principle of compromise and willingness on the part of the contestants to reach a friendly settlement, was clearly shown in the very beginning of the Council's history, in the Aaland Islands case. This was a notable success, achieved by the Council at a time when procedure was undeveloped and precedents not yet set. The Swedish Government was loyal to the ideal of international peaceful settlement, both on general grounds and because of its long and intimate relations with its neighbor Finland. It was willing to accept what seemed to it an unjust Council decision in view of the larger interests involved. With such backing, an international Council can deal with any political issue, no matter how complicated; without it, the problem of pacific settlement becomes one of the threat or actual use of international force in a police action against those threatening to resort to force and violence on their own account—a problem not yet solved by either the League of Nations or the United Nations.

Our study, therefore, lies chiefly in the field where conciliation actually has a chance to work by the good will and good faith of nations. Assuming such an attitude, the question of procedure then becomes of cardinal importance. And here the Council, operating largely under Paragraph Two of Article 11, laid certain solid foundations. Gradually a well-defined pattern began to emerge. A dispute would be submitted, the Council would hear both sides and then urge them to settle their differences through direct negotiation. Should this not prove satisfactory, the Council would appoint a Committee, either of members or nonmembers, whose duty it would be to supervise negotiations and to attempt conciliation of the parties. Only if these procedures proved unsuccessful did the Council actually make a binding decision of substance. The major emphasis, then, was laid on mediation between the parties and the conciliation of their disputes, with sanctions very much in the background, to be used only as a last resort. In so far as it was helpful in the relaxation of international tensions, the Council succeeded because it was an international political tribunal to which appeal was possible, and before which both sides could be thoroughly aired and discussed before the issue grew into insoluble proportions.

RUSSIAN BOMBARDMENT OF PERSIAN PORT
(Articles X and XI: *Official Journal, 1920,* 217)

The first complaint before the Council was brought by Persia against Soviet Russia under Articles X and XI of the Covenant. According to the Persian charge, a Soviet admiral in pursuit of the White Russian, General Anton Denikin, had bombed the Persian port of Enzeli, creating a situation which threatened to disturb the peace of the Middle East. By the time the Council was ready to consider this question on June 16, 1920, direct negotiations between the two countries had already started, resulting in the withdrawal of Soviet forces. There was, therefore, no need of Council discussion.

THE AALAND ISLANDS
(Article XI: *Official Journal, 1920,* 246, 297, 394–397; *1921,* 64, 691–706; *1922,* 90, 124)

The decision of the Council in the case of the Aaland Islands was one of its most successful—a success due largely to the conciliatory spirit shown by the parties involved. The issues concerned—of self-determination and of neutralization—were of vital interest to both Sweden and Finland and were potentially highly explosive.

The background of the case was the following:

The Aaland group consists of about three hundred islands which form a bridge across the mouth of the Gulf of Bothnia between Sweden and Finland. These islands are of great strategic importance and were inhabited after the first World War by approximately twenty-six thousand persons of Swedish descent and culture. At the time of the Finnish declaration of independence the Aaland islanders wanted to unite with Sweden, with which the whole of Finland had been united until 1809. This movement for union with Sweden grew, and although the Finnish Government in 1918 announced measures of autonomy, the political situation became more serious.

The Council of the League received this case on the appeal of Lord Curzon who, in June of 1920, exercised the friendly right of members of the League to bring before it any situation threatening the general peace. (Article XI.) Though the Finnish Government was not even a member of the League and the Swedish Government had no membership on the Council, both were invited to appear and present their cases. The Finnish Government maintained that this was an issue of domestic jurisdiction alone, while the Swedish Government prophesied that conflict between the two countries was very likely should the situation be allowed to continue, and asked for a plebiscite.

The first question to which the Council turned was that of its own competence, which was denied by Finland. Since the World Court was not yet in existence the Council appointed a commission of three international jurists who, in September, 1920, delivered to the Council an advisory opinion to the effect that the dispute was not a domestic one and that the Council was, therefore, competent to consider it. As a result of this opinion, the Council appointed a Committee of Inquiry of three members which, after exhaustive research within the area in dispute, reported in April, 1921, that Finland's right of sovereignty over the Aaland Islands could not be disputed. However, the report also recommended that the fears of the islanders be allayed through the grant of wider autonomy. In addition, the Committee stated that a Convention should be worked out providing for the neutralization of the Aaland Islands. The Council accepted the report of its Committee and appointed one of the Council members to help Sweden and Finland work out a system of guarantees. Although the Swedish representative protested, his government agreed to accept loyally the decision of the Council, and both the guarantees and the neutralization were put into effect.

THE DANGER OF WAR BETWEEN POLAND AND LITHUANIA

(Articles XI and XV: *Official Journal, 1921,* 5–8, 271–279, 764–785, 869–881, 990–1006; *1922,* 132–138, 269–274, 327–338, 488; *1923,* 179–186, 224–229, 237–239, 343–345, 580–586, 664–670; *1924,* 1064–1066)

The danger of war between Poland and Lithuania in 1920 arose over control of Vilna. To the Lithuanians, Vilna was the ancient symbol of their culture and their historic capital, while to the Poles it seemed at times much more conclusive that more than half of the population of the city was Polish. After the defeat of the Russians in

1920 Polish and Lithuanian troops came face to face west of the Curzon Line. In September, 1920, the Polish Government appealed to the Council under Article XI, asking it only to secure a provisional settlement and to prevent any hostilities. The Council thereupon set up a military Commission of Control on the spot. As a result of Council efforts Poland and Lithuania signed an agreement on October 7, 1920, at Suwalki, provisionally fixing the positions of their troops.

That these efforts were insufficient to deal with the situation became clear the very next day when the Polish General Zeligowski suddenly occupied Vilna and established there a so-called "Government of Central Lithuania." In trying to deal with this very difficult situation, the Council proceeded along two parallel lines. The Military Commission of Control continued its on-the-spot activities and set up three neutral zones to separate the opposing forces. In this way it was able to prevent numerous outbreaks of hostility. The League Council then turned to the basic question of the territorial dispute between the two states. Two methods were used by the Council—both of them with little success—the final outcome being determined through the use of force outside of the League.

The first method proposed by the Council was the holding of a plebiscite. This proved to be completely impossible. The second method was that of direct negotiations between the two governments under the presidency of a member of the Council, M. Hymans. Since neither of the two countries involved was willing to accept without reservation his recommendations, the negotiations led to nothing, even though his draft scheme was unanimously adopted by the Council, acting under Article XV, paragraph 4 (September, 1921). In January, 1922, the Council decided to withdraw its Military Commission of Control. In March, 1922, Vilna was incorporated into Poland, and a year later the Conference of Ambassadors finally recognized the "solution" brought about by force and drafted a frontier which assigned the whole city and territory of Vilna to Poland.

COSTA RICA AND PANAMA
(General Principles, no Article: *Official Journal, 1921,* 214–219, 341–344)

In February, 1921, Panama complained to the Council that a Costa Rican detachment had, without provocation, occupied a Panamanian village, which led to a counter-invasion by police and volunteer forces. This conflict was settled through the good offices of the United States of America. The Council was kept informed.

THE ALBANIAN FRONTIER: INVASION BY SERBIANS
(Article XI: *Official Journal, 1921,* 474–484, 722–740, 881–896, 1092–1099, 1182–1215; *1922,* 257–269, 324, 383, 486; *1923,* 113–119, 491–511, 558)

In April, 1921, the Albanian Government brought to the attention of the League the violation of its borders by Serbia and Greece. The Council of the League appealed to the three states to refrain from any inflammatory action but refused to consider the question at that time as the Conference of Ambassadors was then dealing with it. When the Second Assembly met in September, 1921, it asked the Council to appoint an impartial commission of three persons to proceed immediately to Albania, which was done. Before the Commission had time to arrive in Albania, however, the British Government, on November 7, brought the whole question before the Council under Article XI in view of the fact that Yugoslav troops were reported in the northern part of Albania.

The Council met in special session on November 18 and heard representatives of the parties involved. The Conference of Ambassadors informed the Council that on November 9 it had definitely fixed the frontiers of Albania, a decision which the Serb-Croat-Slovene Government stated it was willing to respect. Therefore, the problem became one of evacuation of troops according to the newly established frontier. On December 10 the Council's Commission of Inquiry in Albania reported that evacuation had taken place. Both countries had shown their willingness to abide by an international decision.

THE PARTITION OF UPPER SILESIA
(Article XI: *Official Journal, 1921*, 982–984, 1220–1233; *1922*, 53–56, 88; *1923*, 242, 559)

According to the Treaty of Versailles, a plebiscite was to be held in certain sections of German Upper Silesia for the purposes of providing information from which a just frontier could be drawn between the German and Polish populations of that area. Excitement ran high and both groups engaged in furious propaganda and terroristic activities in an effort to sway the population in one direction or the other, leading to an extremely tense situation. The plebiscite, under the direction of the International Commission, was held in March, 1921, and just as the Commission was about to inform the Supreme Council of its results, a Polish insurrection broke out in Upper Silesia. The Boundary Commission was unable to reach a final conclusion: the plebiscite had returned a German majority in the north and west of the area, a Polish majority in the south and east and had shown the center to be of mixed population. On August 12, 1921, M. Briand, the President of the Supreme Council, informed the League Council that it was transferring the case to it by virtue of Article XI of the Covenant.

As the matter was one of extreme urgency, the Council met on August 29 in extraordinary session and decided that the preliminary investigation should be carried on by representatives of Belgium, Brazil, China and Spain, all States which had not participated in any way in the discussions or investigations which had already taken place. On the basis of the work of the Committee of Four and the work also of experts on the economic organization of Upper Silesia, the Council on October 12 adopted a recommended frontier line, certain transitional measures of an economic nature and clauses relating to rights of nationality and protection of minorities.

The above recommendations were adopted by the Conference of Ambassadors (representing in this case the Supreme Council), and the Council was requested to select some suitable person to preside over necessary German-Polish negotiations.

EASTERN KARELIA
  (Articles XI, XIV and XVII: *Official Journal, 1922,* 104, 107, 165–170;
  1923, 221, 343–345, 572–577, 659–664, 1335)

In October, 1920, the governments of Soviet Russia and Finland had signed the Treaty of Dorpat which provided political, economic and cultural autonomy for Eastern Karelia under Russian sovereignty. In 1921 a rebellion occurred in Eastern Karelia which was severely repressed by the Soviet authorities, and in November, 1921, Finland appealed to the Council under Article XI, claiming that the provisions of the above Treaty were not being observed. Considering the matter in January, 1922, the Council stated that it was willing to investigate the problem provided only that both countries involved would agree to such Council procedure. The Soviet Government, a non-Member of the League, declared that the question of Eastern Karelia was one purely of domestic concern. The Finnish Government then suggested that the Council should, under Article XIV, ask the World Court for an advisory opinion on this point. The Soviet Government categorically refused to take any part in the examination of this question either by the League or by the Court. Therefore, the Court reluctantly stated that it could not express any opinion since it did not have the consent of both parties. The Council was also unable to proceed with the case.

ALLEGED BULGARIAN INCURSIONS INTO BORDERING COUNTRIES
  (Article XI: *Official Journal, 1922,* 795–798, 803–804, 1110–1114, 1133–1134)

In July, 1922, the Bulgarian Government appealed to the Council under Article XI, stating that it had taken steps to cope with the disturbances caused by Bulgarian armed bands which carried out attacks into the frontier districts of countries neighboring Bulgaria. On June 14, however, the Bulgarian Government had received an official note from Rumania, speaking also for Greece and Yugoslavia, in which the three States concerned declared that they held Bulgaria responsible and threatened serious consequences if these attacks were not immediately discontinued. Since the Bulgarian Government felt it could not completely control the armed bands, it appealed to the Council to intervene.

The Council in its discussions took note of the fact that negotiations were proceeding concerning action to be taken to stop these armed attacks and suggested that these negotiations continue.

THE TUNIS NATIONALITY DECREES
(Article XV: *Official Journal, 1922,* 1204, 1206)

In November, 1921, a dispute developed between France and Great Britain concerning the application to British subjects of certain nationality decrees in force in Tunis and in the French zone of Morocco. After long diplomatic correspondence which ended in a deadlock, the British Government, in September, 1922, brought the question before the Council under Article XV of the Covenant. The French Government claimed that the question of its nationality decrees was a purely domestic one. In order to settle this legal point the Council referred the case to the World Court which, in February, 1923, announced that in these particular circumstances the question of nationality decrees had become of international concern.

In May, 1923, a friendly settlement was reached between the two governments through direct negotiations.

EXPROPRIATION BY THE RUMANIAN GOVERNMENT OF THE IMMOVABLE PROPERTY OF HUNGARIAN OPTANTS
(Article XI: *Official Journal, 1923,* 120–122, 573, 604, 703, 729–736, 886, 903–904, 1009–1011)

In March, 1923, the Hungarian Government brought before the League Council a request that it consider under Article XI the question of the expropriation by Rumania of the immovable property of Hungarian optants. After initial discussion by the Council in April, direct negotiations between the two governments were held in Brussels under the supervision of the Japanese representative on the Council. However, since the Hungarian Government did not accept the recommendations which resulted from these negotiations, nothing positive was achieved; and the Council in July, 1923, could do very little other than express a hope that the two countries involved would not allow this issue to go on poisoning their relations.

THE AUSTRO-HUNGARIAN FRONTIER
(Treaty of Trianon: *Official Journal, 1922,* 767, 777; *1923,* 178)

According to the Treaty of Trianon, the district of Burgenland had been assigned to Austria because of its predominantly German population. However, when the time came to give up this territory, the Hungarian Government objected on the ground that it had been Hungarian territory throughout its history. A conference was held at Venice under the auspices of the Italian Government at which it was agreed that a plebiscite should be held in a certain part of the Burgenland. This plebiscite, held in November, 1921, resulted in a majority in favor of Hungary, and the Conference of Ambassadors decided, therefore, to return it to Hungary. Austria objected but, true to the agreement reached at Venice, declared that it would accept any decision which the Council of the League might reach on the subject provided it did so unanimously. The Hungarian Government also agreed to this procedure, and the Conference of Ambassadors requested the Council to give a binding award. In September, 1922, the Council drew up the boundary line in this area which was accepted by both parties.

THE FRONTIER BETWEEN POLAND AND CZECHOSLOVAKIA
(Article XI: *Official Journal, 1923,* 1316, 1332; *1924,* 345, 356–359, 364–369, 398–399, 520–521, 627–630, 828–829)

In August, 1923, the Conference of Ambassadors asked the Council under Article XI to recommend a boundary line between Poland and Czechoslovakia in the Jaworzina district. The Council, after considering the history of this matter, decided to ask for an advisory opinion from the World Court as to whether it was competent to consider this matter. After a favorable reply the Council, in March, 1924, traced the frontier on the basis of new proposals submitted by the Boundary Commission. Both Poland and Czechoslovakia accepted the decision of the Council.

THE MURDER OF GENERAL TELLINI FOLLOWED BY THE BOMBARDMENT OF CORFU
(Articles XII and XV: *Official Journal, 1923*, 1274, 1276, 1286–1290, 1294–1301, 1304–1310, 1313–1316)

The Conference of Ambassadors had appointed a Commission to fix the frontiers of Albania, and it was while discharging this duty that General Tellini, together with his aides, was murdered on August 27, 1923, on Greek territory near the village of Janina. The Greek Government immediately announced its official regrets and pledged the punishment of the criminals. However, patriotic indignation in Mussolini's Italy ran very high and on August 29 an Italian ultimatum was sent to the Greek Government demanding an unreserved official apology, a solemn memorial service for the victims, honors to the Italian flag by the Greek fleet, a drastic inquiry by the Greek authorities at the place of assassination in the presence of an Italian observer, capital punishment for all the authors of the crime as well as an indemnity of 50 million Italian lire and military honors to the bodies of the victims.

The Greek Government replied on the next day in a conciliatory fashion but protesting that the fourth, fifth and sixth demands were unacceptable to it. On August 31 the Italian Government took matters in its own hands—occupying the Island of Corfu after an initial bombardment. According to the Italian Government, this temporary occupation was necessary as a pledge for the reparations which it demanded from Greece.

On September 1, before it had any knowledge of the occupation of Corfu, the Greek Government appealed to the Council under Articles XII and XV, stating that it was ready to carry out in good faith any proposals which the Council would make. However, the Greek Government added that a necessary condition was the cessation of the policy of coercion which the Italian Government was pursuing. The Italian representative maintained that this issue was being dealt with by the Conference of Ambassadors, that it was not properly within the province of the Council and that any discussion of Article XVI (introduced by some Council Members) was out of place, since Italy had definitely stated that it had not intended to commit an act of war.

The actual decision, made in the Conference of Ambassadors and not by the Council, in effect allowed most of the Italian demands. A provision was made for a Greek naval salute to British, French and Italian squadrons, the investigation of the murders by an international commission and the payment by Greece to Italy of 50 million lire. In return the Italians evacuated Corfu. At the time, Members of the Council hailed this development as a resounding success for international organization. Actually, however, since most of the Italian demands had been granted, and since the Italian Government had not had to pay any damages to Greece for the destruction of property and lives in the occupation of Corfu, the so-called settlement of this incident really amounted to admitting that it paid to use force.

THE ADMINISTRATION OF MEMEL
(Article XI: *Official Journal, 1924,* 121–162, 353–356, 361–364, 514–520, 539–543, 598–627, 1220–1224)

In September, 1923, the Conference of Ambassadors brought the question of the administration of Memel before the Council under Article XI. From the Peace Conference until the beginning of 1923 the Memel territory had been administered by a representative of the Allies. In January, 1923, an organized group of Lithuanians seized Memel and established a *de facto* government there. The Conference of Ambassadors immediately sent a Commission of Inquiry to the spot, but it was unable to conduct successful negotiations and the matter was referred to the Council, which immediately appointed a Commission of three members which began investigations in Lithuania, Poland and Memel. When the Council met on March 10, a draft convention was ready for it, the terms of which had been accepted by the Lithuanian Government. After having been adopted by the Council, the convention was sent to the Conference of Ambassadors and was there signed by the Allied Governments and the Lithuanian Government in May, 1924.

THE FRONTIER BETWEEN TURKEY AND IRAQ
(Treaty of Lausanne and Articles XI, XIV and XV: *Official Journal,
1923,* 249; *1924,* 1291, 1337–1358, 1925–1944; *1925,* 1317–1338, 1377–
1383; *1926,* 120–129, 145, 187–193, 548–552)

According to the terms of the Treaty of Lausanne, the frontier
between Turkey and Iraq was to have been laid down by direct
negotiations between Turkey and Britain. These negotiations proved
unsuccessful, however. The British Government, therefore, submitted the dispute to the Council in August, 1924. The Council,
meeting in September, decided to set up a special committee of
three (non-Members) which was to proceed to the disputed area
and there conduct its investigations. Both governments were to refrain from any action which might change the situation in the
disputed territory until such time as the Council had reached a decision; in order to carry out this last provision, the Council drew up
a provisional boundary defining the territory to be occupied and
administered by each party pending the establishment of the final
boundary.

After two months of investigation in Mosul the Commission drew
up a report which it presented to the Council in September, 1925.
After hearing the observations of the British and Turkish representatives, the Council decided to appoint a committee of three of its own
Members for the purpose of reconciling the two parties and working
out a settlement by mediation. This, however, proved impossible.
On the suggestion of its committee the Council then proceeded to
ask the World Court for an opinion on the character of the decision
which it was to take and also whether that decision had to be
unanimous or not. In answer to this request the Court stated that
the power of binding decision was in the hands of the Council of
the League and that as far as method was concerned, the principle
of unanimity in voting was in this case modified by the fact that
votes cast by representatives of interested parties were not to be
counted.

After receiving this opinion, the Council made a final unsuccessful
effort at mediation, and then on December 16 gave its decision.
The frontier was fixed largely according to the proposals of the

British Government, that is, the region of Mosul was declared to be part of Iraq. This decision was conditional on the continuation of the British mandate in Iraq for twenty-five years, unless the government of Iraq was admitted into the League of Nations as a member before the expiration of the twenty-five years. On June 5, 1926, an agreement was signed between England and Turkey which settled their conflict according to the terms of the Council's decision.

THE MONASTERY OF SAINT NAOUM
("Precedent," Article XIV: *Official Journal,* 1924, 909–910, 919–920, 1309)

In December, 1922, the Conference of Ambassadors assigned to Albania the region around the Monastery of Saint Naoum, a decision which the government of the Serb-Croat-Slovene Kingdom wished to be reconsidered. The Conference referred the issue to the Council "in accordance with precedent," and the Council, in turn, referred it to the World Court for an advisory opinion. In October, 1924, the advisory opinion of the Court was sent to the Conference of Ambassadors, with a request from the Council that it finish the task of delimiting the frontiers as soon as possible.

GRECO-TURKISH EXCHANGE OF NATIONALS
(Articles XI and XIV: *Official Journal,* 1923, 1312; 1924, 324, 764, 1066–1069; 1925, 441; 1926, 153–158; 1927, 622–625; 1928, 369, 403, 453, 867, 1487)

In October, 1924, the Greek Government requested the Council to place on its agenda, under Article XI, the question of the Greek minority in Constantinople. The charge brought to the attention of the Council the fact that the Commission, which had been created in 1923 to supervise the exchange of populations between Greece and Turkey, had suspended its sessions because of a difference as to interpretation of the word "established" as it was used in the 1923 convention. The Council referred this matter to the World Court for an advisory opinion.

EXPULSION OF THE OECUMENICAL PATRIARCH
(Article XI: *Official Journal, 1925,* 482–484, 487–489, 578–581, 637–640, 854, 895)

On February 11, 1925, the Greek Government telegraphed the Secretary-General, charging that the expulsion by Turkish authorities from Constantinople of the Oecumenical Patriarch was a serious infringement of the Lausanne Agreement concerning the constitution and activities of the Patriarchate and appealing for the consideration by the Council under Article XI.

On June 1 the Greek Government informed the Council that negotiations with Turkey had been successfully concluded. As a result the matter was withdrawn from the Council agenda, and an earlier request for an advisory World Court opinion was also made unnecessary.

THE GRECO-BULGARIAN DISPUTE
(Articles X, XI and XII: *Official Journal, 1926,* 108–118, 172–174, 196–211, 580–585, 1403; *1927,* 396, 732–735, 1417)

On October 19, 1925, Greek and Bulgarian sentries exchanged shots at a border point north-east of Salonika. A Greek sentry and a Greek officer were killed, and prolonged firing ensued. The Bulgarian Government proposed a mixed commission to investigate the incident, but the Greek Government demanded apologies and reparations and ordered its troops to advance into the valley of the Struma River. On October 22, the Bulgarian Government called on the Council by virtue of Articles X and XI. Before the Council had time to meet, its President, M. Briand, appreciating the importance of immediate action, sent a telegram to both parties reminding them of their obligations under Article XII and asking both to withdraw their troops behind the frontiers. Both governments agreed to carry out this appeal, which arrived only two-and-a-half hours before a Greek offensive had been scheduled to begin.

On October 26 the Council met in hastily summoned session and approved of Briand's step. The first problem was to ensure that hostilities would not start and for this purpose the Council sent its famous and highly successful "stop-fight" resolution to the two states, asking them to withdraw all their forces behind the frontiers within sixty hours. A military commission was sent to supervise the retirement of the forces and was able to report on the 29th of October that the frontier was calm and that both nations were complying with the Council resolution.

It was now up to the Council to attack the second part of its task —which was the determination of responsibility. On the 29th of October the Council decided to appoint a five-man Commission of Inquiry to conduct an on-the-spot investigation together with the military commission appointed earlier. On the basis of this investigation, it was decided that the Greek occupation of Bulgaria had violated the Covenant of the League of Nations, and Greece was obliged to pay an indemnity of approximately $210,000.

THE FRONTIER BETWEEN GREECE AND TURKEY
(Articles XI and XIV: *Official Journal, 1926*, 511–516, 529–590)

In February, 1926, Greece brought before the Council, by virtue of Article XI, a dispute with Turkey concerning the demarcation of the Maritza Delta frontier, requesting the Council to get an advisory opinion from the Court (Article XIV). Instead, the Council requested the jurists attached to delegations then present at Geneva to make a report. The gist of the report was that this was not a proper matter for the Council to deal with under Article XI.

LITHUANIAN-POLISH RELATIONS
(No Article. *Official Journal, 1926, 507*)

In February, 1926, Lithuania protested to the Council concerning the alleged occupation by Polish forces of Lithuanian territory near Kernovo. No discussion took place in the Council because the particular incidents were settled through direct negotiation.

THE PROPERTY OF HUNGARIAN OPTANTS IN RUMANIA
(Article XI, Article 239 of Treaty of Trianon: *Official Journal, 1928*, 110, 407–430, 436–446, 1454–1470, 1947–1950; *1929*, 504, 977; *1930*, 85, 498)

Both the Rumanian and Hungarian Governments asked for the intervention of the Council under Article XI (February, 1927) to decide certain issues concerning the Mixed Arbitral Tribunal which dealt with the immovable property of Hungarian optants. The Council appointed a Committee of Three which recommended that the Rumanian judge on the Tribunal be reinstated, a recommendation which proved unacceptable to the Hungarian Government.

In March, 1928, the problem of the property of Hungarian optants was brought to the Council for the third time. The Council again urged compromise.

THE SZENT-GOTTHARD ARMS INCIDENT
(Dispute not under the Covenant. *Official Journal, 1928,* 387, 452, 904–919)

On January 1, 1928, a shipment of machine gun parts, falsely declared, was seized by Austrian customs officials at the joint Austro-Hungarian frontier station of Szent-Gotthard, on Hungarian territory. The Hungarian Government had not issued a permit for the transit of these goods, and on February 1, the Czechoslovak, Rumanian and Yugoslav Governments asked the Council to intervene under its decisions of September 27, 1924, and December 11, 1926, defining the exercise of its right of investigation under Article 143 of the Trianon Treaty. Sale of the material at auction by Hungarian authorities was halted after an appeal by the acting president of the Council.

The Council heard the parties on March 7 and appointed a Committee of Three which, on March 10, asked that technical experts chosen by the League be sent to the spot. They reported on June 7. The Council resolution noted that the final destination of the arms had not been determined and regretted that Hungry had considered the incident only from the standpoint of railway and customs regulations and had not taken into account the obligation to prohibit trade in arms—an obligation which resulted from the Treaty of Trianon.

THE ALBANIAN MINORITY IN GREECE
(Article XI: *Official Journal, 1928,* 868–877, 883, 942–945)

On May 9, 1928, Albania appealed to the Council under Article XI of the Covenant and on June 5 listed fifteen charges against the

Greek Government affecting the property of Albanians and the Moslem Albanian minority in Chamuria.

The Council sent the matter to a Committee of Three, and on June 9 adopted a report under which it refused to consider such an appeal based on Article XI. It stated that the consideration of such complaints should take place under the regular minority procedure or by direct negotiation between the parties. Article XI, the Council asserted, was intended for grave cases. Its use in more or less normal cases would create the very dangers which the minorities treaties were designed to avoid.

LITHUANIAN-POLISH RELATIONS, 1927–1931

(Article XI: *Official Journal, 1928,* 144–156, 176–178, 779–792, 833–838, 893–897; *1929,* 21–31, 44–47, 1325–1330; *1930,* 824, 1501–1502, 1783–1784)

On October 15, 1927, Lithuania requested the Council to consider its relations with Poland under Article XI of the Covenant; on the 26th, Lithuania made a further request concerning the expulsion of eleven Polish nationals into "independent Lithuania" and issues concerning the status of schools, teachers and clergy in Vilna and Grodno. Lithuania referred to relations between Poland and Lithuania as a state of war.

The Council heard the heads of both governments on December 7 and appointed a frontier mission of three military attachés to investigate on the spot. On the 10th it adopted a report according to which the exiled Polish nationals were allowed to return to Vilna, and the other complaints were to be referred to a Committee of the Council. According to the Council resolution, the two governments were to enter into direct negotiations as soon as possible to establish satisfactory relations, for which purpose the good offices of the League were at their disposal. Political tensions were eased temporarily but negotiations led to nothing, and on September 2, 1928, the Council decided to look after the interests of third parties if the two did not agree on such matters as local traffic, transit and postal communication.

A provisional agreement granting minor frontier traffic privileges was signed on November 7, 1928. On September 18, 1930, the Council passed on to the two parties a report concerning provision for the establishment of free communications between them. An advisory opinion was given by the Court on a minor legal point. Relations between Poland and Lithuania continued unimproved.

BULGARIA AND GREECE; THE RHODOPE FORESTS
(Dispute not under the Covenant. *Official Journal, 1933,* 799; *1934,* 1432)

A company organized before the war to exploit the Rhodope forests was dispossessed under a Bulgarian decree in 1918, and certain interested Greeks appealed to their government. In 1926 Bulgaria granted to a foreign company a concession which included the disputed forests. Greece decided to ask for a decision by arbitration under Article 181 of the Treaty of Neuilly and on July 15, 1930, called on the Council to appoint the arbitrator.

The Council heard the parties on September 24 and appointed as arbitrator, Osten Unden (on October 2). Pursuant to the decision of a committee of jurists upon which the Council had called, the arbitrator was given the power to decide both on the receivability and the substance of the issues involved.

On March 23, 1933, the arbitrator rendered an award on the substance of the dispute. The execution of the award was reviewed by the Council on September 19, 1934, at the request of Greece.

THE SINO-JAPANESE DISPUTE
(Articles X, XI, XV and XVI. Referred to Assembly under Article XV: *Official Journal, 1931,* 2248, 2265–2274, 2279–2285, 2289–2293, 2307–2309, 2309–2358, 2362–2364, 2364–2371, 2374–2383, 2451–2493; *1932,* 283–306, 326–428, 917–944, 1869–1915; *1933,* 1062–1063)

MUKDEN

After the incident of September 18, 1931, China addressed an appeal to the Council under Article XI, choosing that Article largely because the Council already had a well-established procedure under it. On September 21, 1931, the Council issued an ineffective stop-fight order.

On September 30, by unanimous vote, the Council requested both parties to restore normal relations and to keep the Council informed of developments. No impartial committee of inquiry was established at this time, largely because of United States and British opposition.

In the meantime, after disastrous initial hesitation, the American Government decided to back the League and on October 9, Secretary Henry L. Stimson informed the League that the United States would try to help, by means of independent diplomatic steps. When the Council reconvened, it was decided to invite an American representative. The Japanese objected but it was held that this was a procedural matter not requiring unanimity. Mr. Prentiss Gilbert was instructed, however, to discuss only issues connected with the Kellogg Pact. On October 17 the Council invoked the Pact of Paris; on October 20 the United States formally invoked the Pact of Paris in identical notes to China and Japan. On October 24 the Council passed a second resolution calling on Japan to begin at once the withdrawal of its troops, the process to be finished by November 16, and asking China to assume responsibility for the safety of Japanese subjects. As soon as evacuation was completed, direct negotiations were to begin. This decision had no legal effect, as the Japanese delegate voted against it, thus destroying the unanimity required under Article XI.

As is well known, fighting in Manchuria continued. On November 21 Japan proposed that the Council appoint a commission of inquiry, and on December 10 the Council, meeting now without an American representative, unanimously and belatedly voted to send such a body. It was appointed in January, 1932, and reached the Far East at the end of February.

Meanwhile the military situation deteriorated with the Japanese advancing to the Great Wall. The anti-Japanese boycott gathered strength. In Manchuria the Japanese set up a puppet government.

SHANGHAI

The Council reassembled at the end of January, and on January 29, Japan attacked Shanghai. The Chinese representative immediately invoked Articles X and XV and later Article XVI. The Secretary-General appointed a consular committee of investigation at Shanghai, acting under League supervision. They reported on February 12 that a state of open war existed and that the Japanese aimed to drive the Chinese out of the city. On the 12th of February also, China asked the Council to refer the dispute to the Assembly under Article XV, paragraph 9. On February 16 twelve Council members (not including China and Japan) called on Tokyo to remind the Japanese Government that under Article X no infringement of the territorial integrity and political independence of any member of the League could be recognized as valid. On February 19 the Council summoned an extraordinary session of the Assembly to meet March 3.

THE ASSEMBLY CONSIDERS THE ISSUES

On March 4 the Assembly unanimously called on the Japanese to withdraw from Shanghai; on March 11 it subscribed to the Stimson Doctrine (of January 7) and created a Committee of Nineteen to report on the ending of hostilities and Japanese withdrawal and to prepare a settlement of the dispute. Little was contributed to the Assembly discussion by the Great Powers, who were fearful of the responsibilities which might be imposed on them by sanctions. On May 5 an armistice was signed and the Japanese withdrew from Shanghai. In Geneva a resolution was passed unanimously in the Assembly, providing for the nonrecognition of the Manchurian puppet government by all League members.

On November 21, 1932, the Council began considering the Lytton Report, and in December it referred it to a special session of the Assembly. On December 9 the Assembly referred the report to the Committee of Nineteen (members of the Council other than the parties, plus six members elected by the Assembly by secret ballot; these were Switzerland, Czechoslovakia, Colombia, Portugal, Hungary and Sweden). On December 15 the Committee of Nineteen proposed the transfer of the question to a conciliatory body, of its own members and representatives of the United States and the U.S.S.R. This was rejected by Japan. On December 20 the Committee adjourned with the hope of persuading Japan to accept its plan.

On February 17, 1933, the Committee reported to the Assembly, recommending a solution along the lines of the Lytton Report. This was accepted unanimously by the Assembly on February 24, and the Japanese delegate withdrew from the League. The Assembly set up an Advisory Committee to follow the developments; no sanction other than nonrecognition was suggested.

In May, 1933, the Tangku Truce was signed, by which China agreed to demilitarize five thousand square miles on the Chinese side of the Great Wall. The Japanese victory was complete.

LETICIA: PERU AND COLOMBIA
(Article IV, paragraph 4, not specified. Article XV: *Official Journal,*
1933, 117, 183, 195, 253–263, 265–269, 492–525, 527–614, 621–626,
631–633, 1107–1110; *1934,* 19–26, 283–288, 874–938; *1935,* 443–447,
1647; *1938,* 117–125, 242, 306–309, 378–380, 533–535, 618–622, 665–
669, 803, 988–989, 1133–1144)

On September 22, 1932, a group of Peruvians entered the upper Amazon port of Leticia, capital of a district which Peru had recognized as belonging to Colombia in a treaty signed in 1922. On January 4, 1933, Colombia informed the Secretary-General of the situation and ten days later, after Colombia had sent troops to Leticia, the President of the Council sent the equivalent of a stopfight resolution to both sides. Answers were received from both parties.

On January 24 the Council approved of the action of its President and requested the Committee which was already dealing with the Bolivia-Paraguay conflict (see below) to follow the Leticia dispute. The Committee was composed of representatives of Spain, Guatemala and the Irish Free State. On the 26th the Council sent telegrams to both sides asking them to refrain from violations of each other's territory.

On February 3 the Council heard representatives of both parties and informed Peru that it could not agree that it had any right to resist the re-establishment of Colombian authority. The Council Committee of Three was instructed to follow developments. Relations deteriorated, and on February 18 Colombia asked that the Council be convened to examine Peruvian aggression under Article XV, to restore the *status quo* and to decide the nature and extent of the reparation which Peru should pay.

The Council met on February 21, 1933; Peru refused to attend. The Council requested its Committee of Three to seek a settlement, a procedure which received the strong backing of the United States. The disputants agreed to immediate cessation of hostilities. On March 1 the Committee of Three reported to the Council recommending that the territory be evacuated by Peruvian forces and placed under a League Commission which should have an international militia at its disposal. The parties were urged to begin immediate negotiations, with the Council standing by ready to extend good offices. The Council and Colombia accepted this report, but Peru, after suggesting alternative methods, left the meeting at which the report was unanimously adopted. The Council called for Peruvian evacuation followed by negotiations and appointed an Advisory Committee to help in the settlement; Britain, China, Czechoslovakia, France, Germany, Guatemala, Ireland, Italy, Mexico, Norway, Panama, Poland and Spain, with the United States and Brazil invited to participate, formed this Committee.

On May 10, 1933, the Committee recommended that the Council's recommendation of March 18 be accepted; that the Council send a commission to Leticia to take charge of the area; that Peruvian forces withdraw immediately upon the arrival of the Commission; and that both cease hostilities, keep their forces within the borders and inform the Advisory Committee of the progress of discussions. This was accepted by both parties on May 25, 1933.

The Council now appointed a commission of three (the United States, Brazil and Spain), which arrived in Leticia on June 23. On May 24, 1934, a protocol of peace, friendship and co-operation was signed. On June 19, 1934, the League Commission handed over the "Leticia Trapezium" to the civil authorities of Colombia.

THE BULGARIAN AND GREEK DEBTS
(Dispute not under the Covenant. *Official Journal, 1931,* 2059–2069, 2261; *1932,* 1185–1187)

After the incident of 1925, Greece and Bulgaria had concluded under League auspices the Caphandaris-Molloff agreement of 1927 to provide for liquidating claims of exchanged emigrants. Greece did not make the July, 1931, payment, claiming that it could set it off against the Bulgarian reparation debt, included in the Hoover moratorium on intergovernmental debts. Bulgaria on August 7 asked the Council to act under Article 8 of the 1927 agreement and settle the difference of interpretation.

The Council heard the parties and asked for an advisory opinion from the Court. The parties reached a *modus vivendi* in November, 1931. The Court held that there was no dispute within Article 8 of the 1927 agreement as the powers of the Court did not extend to interpretation of the Hoover moratorium.

The Council heard the parties in May, 1932, and expressed hope for a satisfactory settlement of the difficulty.

GRAN CHACO
(Article IV, Articles X and XIII, Articles X and XI, Articles XV and XVI: *Official Journal, 1929,* 21, 56, 71–73, 253–255, 264–273, 877–879; *1930,* 261–266, 538; *1933,* 373–381, 849, 1061, 1333, 1555–1556, 1557–1593, 1606; *1934,* 242–272, 507–508, 520–522, 639–644, 748–767, 768, 866; *1935,* 124, 447–452, 900–909, 985–989, 1648–1657; *1936,* 279, 925; *1937,* 261)

On December 5, 1928, Paraguayan forces attacked a Bolivian fort. Although the matter was not brought before the Council by any State, on December 11, 1928, the Council unanimously requested its President to send a cable to both parties. This was done, and Bolivia and Paraguay were reminded of their obligations under the Covenant (Article IV).

After preliminary correspondence, Bolivia on December 14 denounced Paraguay and invoked Articles X and XIII. The League Council took no further steps, viewing with approval the efforts of an inter-American Commission of Investigation and Conciliation. There was no danger of hostilities at this time, but the Commission was unable to arrive at a satisfactory formula. On June 15, 1932, fighting broke out again. The Washington negotiations (now being conducted by a Committee of Neutrals) broke up.

On August 1 Paraguay appealed to the League under Articles X and XI, following receipt of a note from the Council expressing hope for peace. Again the Council took a "back seat," preferring to see a settlement through local means. Numerous proposals were made, to no avail. On September 23 the Council met in regular session. M. Madariaga pointed out that the Covenant was the only treaty binding the disputants to settle their disputes pacifically, as Bolivia had not ratified the Kellogg Pact. The Council limited itself to the appointment of a committee to follow the efforts of the Committee of Neutrals.

After further fruitless negotiations in Washington, the Committee of Three suggested that the Committee of Neutrals in Washington send a Military Commission to arrange a truce. This the Council recommended on November 25, 1932. On February 3, 1933, the Committee of Three suggested that the Council itself send an investigating body to the Chaco to report. On May 10 Paraguay formally declared war on Bolivia, which invoked Article XVI in an appeal to the Council. After numerous delays the Council Commission proceeded to South America in October. It was able to arrange a temporary armistice from December 19 to December 30 and an extension to January 6, 1934, but was unable to prevent resumption of hostilities. On February 22 it submitted a draft treaty which neither party was willing to accept.

On May 31 Bolivia invoked Article XV as a means of blocking a proposed arms embargo. The Council itself took no formal action. On June 9 Bolivia requested the transfer of the issue to the Assembly. On November 24, 1934, the Assembly adopted a report under Article XV submitted by its Advisory Committee, which recommended that a Neutral Supervisory Commission be set up to arrange a cessation of hostilities on the basis of a mutual evacuation of a "security zone" at the front. In November, 1934, the arms embargo, participated in by most League Members and by the United States, went into effect on the recommendation of the League Commission. Because Paraguay rejected the Report, the Assembly asked that the arms embargo be lifted from Bolivia, and Paraguay withdrew from the League on February 23, 1935.

No further League steps were taken in connection with this dispute. In October, 1938, an arbitral award assigned to Paraguay virtually the entire Chaco zone.

THE AUSTRO-GERMAN CUSTOMS UNION
(Dispute not under the Covenant. *Official Journal, 1931,* 1068–1081, 1160–1172)

On March 19, 1931, the German and Austrian Governments signed a protocol for the establishment of a customs union.

On April 10, 1931, the British Government submitted to the Council the question of the compatibility of the agreement with the terms of Protocol 1 of October 4, 1922, of Article 88 of the Treaty of St. Germain, and of the Austrian Government's pledge not to compromise its independence in any manner.

On the 19th of May the Council agreed to ask for an advisory opinion. This was handed down on September 5, 1931, and it pronounced against the proposed agreement. On September 3, however, the German and Austrian Governments had already stated that they did not intend to go on with the original plan.

On September 7 the Council noted the advisory opinion and also the German statement. The item was dropped.

THE REQUISITIONED FINNISH SHIPS
(Article XI, paragraph 2: *Official Journal, 1931,* 2249–2293; *1932,* 506–510, 1197–1199; *1934,* 522, 1450; *1935,* 181, 418, 433–441, 628–630, 643)

On July 30, 1931, the Finnish Government submitted to the Council under the Covenant its dispute with the United Kingdom concerning Finnish vessels used by the latter during the war. The discussion in the Council centered around the question of its jurisdiction, and on January 30, 1932, it was decided that the difference was not within Articles XII and XV nor did the United Kingdom have to submit it—as to exhaustion of means of recourse—to arbitration or judicial settlement under Article XIII. It was felt, however, that the case could come under Article XI, paragraph 2, of the Covenant, by which the Council was competent to conciliate.

On May 10, 1932, the British proposed and the Finns agreed that the question of remedies available in British law be examined by an arbitrator; in May, 1934, the arbitrator pronounced that Finnish shipowners had exhausted the means of recourse provided by British law.

In January, 1935, the Council instructed a Committee of Three to report not on the legal issue but on the question of expediency. On September 13 the report to the Council was made; the Committee did not deny that the Council could deal with the Finnish application, but it pointed out that the Council could only exercise conciliation. However, the Committee had reached the conclusion that the discussions had provided no basis for recommending a solution. This report was adopted.

THE DISMISSAL OF A MEMEL OFFICIAL
(Dispute not under the Covenant. *Official Journal, 1932,* 529–547, 904–909)

Germany, on February 8, 1932, brought to the attention of the Council under Article 17 of the 1924 Convention the deposition of the President of the Memel Directorate by the Governor of Memel Territory because of a journey the Governor had made to Berlin. The report made to the Council by its legal advisers was inconclusive. However, the parties to the 1924 Convention themselves instituted proceedings for an advisory opinion, which was delivered on August 11, 1932. Lithuania's intervention as regarded appointment of the Directorate was upheld by the Court, but its dissolution of the Diet was condemned.

THE HUNGARIAN-YUGOSLAV FRONTIER INCIDENTS
(Article XI, paragraph 2: *Official Journal, 1934,* 657, 682–737)

On May 12, 1934, Hungary asked the Council to put the question of incidents on the Yugoslav border on its agenda under Article XI, paragraph 2. The Council, having heard mutual grievances on June 5, suggested unanimously that the parties reach a direct agreement. This was done in July of 1934.

TERRORISM ON THE HUNGARIAN-YUGOSLAV FRONTIER
(Article XI, paragraph 2 and Article X: *Official Journal, 1935,* 138, 145, 650, 873)

After the assassination of Barthou and King Alexander in October, 1934, by an agent of Ustasa, a Croatian revolutionary society, Yugoslavia, on November 22 requested the Council under Article XI, paragraph 2, to inquire into the responsibility of Hungary with regard to abetting terroristic activities by Yugoslav subjects which led to the tragedy. Czechoslovakia and Rumania joined in the request.

On December 11 the Council unanimously passed a resolution which condemned the assassinations and insisted on the punishment of those responsible. It also stated every State's duty under Article X to prevent and repress terrorist activity with a political purpose. Furthermore, the Council found that certain Hungarian authorities had been negligent and asked the Hungarian Government to communicate to the Council punitive action it took against them, should their fault be established. A committee of experts was also set up to draw up a draft of an international convention to assure the repression of conspiracies or crimes committed with a political and terrorist purpose.

On January 16, 1935, Hungary submitted a report in which it was shown that the government was not responsible and that certain officials had been punished. The Council on May 25, with the approval of all parties, declared the incident closed.

THE IRAQ-IRANIAN FRONTIER
(Article XI, paragraph 2: *Official Journal, 1935,* 113–117, 118–124, 190–191, 650, 1204)

On November 29, 1934, the Iraq Government appealed against Iran to the Council under Article XI, paragraph 2, of the Covenant. The question at issue was Iraq's access to the sea by the Shattal-Arab, formed by the junction of the Euphrates and Tigris, the whole channel of which was under the control of Iran up to Basra, Iraq's only port. Involved were treaties going as far back as 1847. The Council considered this question in meetings in January and May, 1935. In September the two countries informed the Council that negotiations were proceeding favorably. The Council thereupon adjourned the matter.

THE ITALO-ETHIOPIAN DISPUTE
(Articles XI and XV; Articles XVI and XII; Assembly associated with Council in consideration of sanctions: *Official Journal, 1935,* 124, 162, 248–252, 571–578, 639–643, 720–760, 964–976, 1201–1203, 1209–1227, 1350, 1632; *1936,* 24–47, 240–259, 358–488, 539–540, 572–661, 772–783, 1408–1411; *1937,* 268; *1938,* 10–11, 333–347, 535–551, 669)

On December 13, 1934, following Italy's refusal to arbitrate the Wal-Wal incident, Ethiopia made her first plea to Geneva. On January 3, 1935, Ethiopia requested the Secretary-General to take steps under Article XI to preserve peace. On January 15 Ethiopia asked the Council to request Italy to refrain from further aggression. Not until January 19 did the Secretary-General bring the Ethiopian communication before the Council, which merely voted a resolution pointing out the obligations of the parties as signatories to the 1928 treaty of arbitration. On March 17 Ethiopia informed the Secretary-General that Italy refused arbitration and was preparing for war. She, therefore, laid the dispute before the Council under Article XV and agreed to accept any arbitral award or League recommendation.

The Council continued to press for arbitration, and did not pass a stop-fight resolution. During the arbitral proceeding Ethiopia appealed repeatedly to the Council for action under Article XV. On June 19 Ethiopia informed the Secretary-General that Italy was still sending troops and provoking incidents and asked the Council to appoint neutral observers to visit the frontier districts. No action was taken. The Council decided in favor of Italy's contention that the Wal-Wal incident be excluded from the discussions of the arbitral tribunal.

On July 31 the Council adjourned to permit Britain and France to find a "formula." No formula resulted.

The Council reassembled on September 4 and appointed a Committee of Five (Britain, France, Spain, Poland and Turkey) for the purpose of examining Italo-Ethiopian relations. On September 18 this Committee suggested that Ethiopia should accept foreign advisers in her public services. Italy rejected this proposal together with a British proposal for an exchange of territory. On September 26 the Council finally resolved that it had been acting under Article XV since September 4 and appointed a Committee of Thirteen to draft a report. The Committee met on September 27, and five days later the Italian invasion started. On October 5 the Council reassembled to hear the Committee's report, which refuted Italian charges against Ethiopia. M. Tecla Hawariati asked for action under Article XVI. The Council appointed a Committee of Six which reported that the "Council has come to the conclusion that the Italian Government has resorted to war in disregard of its covenants under Article XII of the Covenant. . . ."

On October 7, 1935, the Council, with Italy in the negative, adopted a report of the Committee of Thirteen. All members also agreed with the report of the Committee of Six. At the Assembly meeting of October 9 all members except Italy, Albania, Austria and Hungary accepted the Council's conclusions and subsequently voted to apply sanctions. On October 11 the Assembly adjourned, and a small Committee of Eighteen was appointed to propose sanctions.

On December 13, the Hoare-Laval plan was communicated to the Council, which merely thanked the British and French Governments for their suggestions and requested its Committee of Thirteen to examine the situation as a whole. On January 23, 1936, the Committee of Thirteen adopted a unanimous report, accepted by the Council, denying international investigation or financial assistance to Ethiopia. Hitler's Rhineland coup destroyed all hope of action against Italy (March 7, 1936). The Committee of Thirteen continued meeting. On May 11 the Council met and passed all responsibility on to the Assembly convoked on the call of Argentina. There also Ethiopia was deserted.

THE REARMAMENT OF GERMANY
(Article XI: *Official Journal, 1935,* 550, 556–565, 569–571)

On March 20, 1935, the French Government, relying on Article XI, paragraph 2, referred to the Council the situation created by the German decision of March 16 to reintroduce general compulsory military service in the Reich and to create a German military air force.

The French application was considered at an extraordinary session of the Council, held from April 15 to 17, and on the 17th a resolution submitted by the French, United Kingdom and Italian representatives was unanimously adopted. (The Danish representative abstained.) This resolution declared that by the unilateral promulgation of the military law of March 16, 1935, the German Government conferred upon itself no right; and condemned the unilateral repudiation of international obligations by the German Government. The Council also invited the British and French Governments which, with the approval of the Italian Government, had sent to the German Government as early as February 3 a plan for a general settlement for the organization of security in Europe and a general limitation of armaments in a system of equality of rights, to continue the negotiations so initiated. The Council also appointed a Committee of Thirteen to propose measures to make the Covenant more effective in the organization of collective security and to define in particular the economic and financial measures which might be applied, should in the future any state endanger peace by unilateral repudiation of international obligations.

RELATIONS BETWEEN THE U.S.S.R. AND URUGUAY
(Article XI: *Official Journal, 1936,* 90–106, 137, 232–240, 503)

On January 4, 1936, the Soviet Government informed the Secretary-General of the suspension of diplomatic relations with Uruguay.

Since no complaint had been made by the Uruguayan Government, the Soviet considered this action a breach of Article XII, paragraph 1. In accordance with Article XI, paragraph 2, the Soviet drew the attention of the Council to this matter.

The Council appointed a Committee of Three to submit a report which was adopted on January 24. In its terms the Council expressed its hope that the difficulty between the two countries would prove to be temporary and that the two parties would refrain from any act which might be harmful to the interests of peace and to the resumption of diplomatic relations in the near future.

THE ISSUE OF THE LOCARNO TREATY
(Dispute not under the Covenant. *Official Journal, 1936*, 311–325, 325, 326–348)

On March 8, 1936, France and Belgium informed the Secretary-General that the German Government had on the 7th notified them that it no longer regarded itself as bound by the Locarno Treaty of Mutual Guarantee. On the same day German troops had entered the demilitarized zone.

On March 14 the Council met in extraordinary session in London. The German Government was invited to send a representative and did so, in the person of von Ribbentrop. Germany was charged with violation of Article 43 of the Versailles Treaty and Article 1 of Locarno.

On March 19 the Council unanimously voted to accept a resolution (Chile abstaining) to the effect that Germany had committed a breach of the above treaties.

THE SPANISH APPEAL
(Article XI: *Official Journal, 1937*, 8–21, 320–322, 914–919, 945–946, 1163–1166; *1938*, 325–332, 354–359, 533, 882–884, 1147–1149)

On December 12, 1936, after a desperate appeal from Spain, the Council passed a feeble resolution affirming that "every State is under an obligation to refrain from intervening in the internal affairs of another State. . . ." In December, 1937, a resolution calling for the end of nonintervention failed.

ALEXANDRETTA AND ANTIOCH
(Article XI: *Official Journal, 1937,* 22–30, 31–34, 36–55, 118–124, 287–289, 312, 837–844; *1938,* 131–153, 622–637)

On December 8, 1936, the Turkish Government asked that in virtue of Article XI of the Covenant there be placed on the agenda of the Council's extraordinary session a dispute which had arisen between Turkey and France concerning the future of the Sanjak of Alexandretta and Antioch. According to the Turkish claim, this area had been conditionally ceded to Turkey by the treaties of 1921 and 1923.

On December 14 Council discussions began, and on December 16 a resolution was proposed to the Council by its *Rapporteur,* M. Sandler of Sweden, in which it was noted that France and Turkey had agreed to postpone to the Council's ordinary session in January the examination of the substance of the question; and also that the two governments had indicated that they would spare no effort to arrive at a satisfactory conclusion. In response to the request of the French Government, it was decided to send three observers to the Sanjak of Alexandretta. This resolution was adopted, the Turkish representative abstaining.

The Council, thus having postponed the examination of the substance of the question to its January session, recommended that the two governments continue their conversations in the meantime, in close contact with the *Rapporteur,* M. Sandler. This was done without successful results, and the two governments continued their discussions through diplomatic channels. Further conversations in the presence of the *Rapporteur* were resumed in Geneva on January 20, 1937, and on January 27 a report agreed to by both parties was submitted to the Council. The Report was adopted by the Council, which then proceeded to appoint a Committee of Experts to draft the Statute and Fundamental Law of the Sanjak, which was to be considered a separate entity with full independence in internal affairs, while the conduct of foreign affairs was to be entrusted to the Government of Syria. Supervision by the Council was to take the form of a delegate on the spot, of French nationality, appointed by the Council. The decisions of the Council were to be taken by a two-thirds majority, without including the parties concerned.

It was provided also that the first elections to the Sanjak Assembly were to be organized by a Commission appointed by the Council. This Commission, established on October 4, 1937, undertook on the spot investigation and elaborated a system of rules of electoral procedure. The execution of its program was, however, delayed as the Turkish Government made certain reservations, and the issue was placed on the agenda of the Council for January, 1938.

On January 31 the Council agreed to set up another committee, of representatives from Belgium, the United Kingdom, France, Sweden and Turkey; this committee was to make modifications in the rules for election. In March of 1938 this Council Committee unanimously adopted electoral regulations and fixed July 15, 1938, as the date by which elections were to be completed. The Electoral Commission proceeded to the Sanjak, began the registration of voters, but felt it had to stop; on July 3, 1938, France and Turkey concluded a pact under which Turkish troops were to participate in the policing of the Sanjak during the election of a local constituent assembly. After this, the League had nothing to say in the settlement of this issue. On June 23, 1939, France and Turkey signed a pact by which the area was ceded to Turkey. It must be noted that the territory did not belong to France to cede, as a mandatory has no legal title to the area which it supervises.

CHINA—1937–1938

(Articles X, XI and XVII; Referred to Assembly; Article XVI: *Official Journal, 1938,* 117–125, 242, 306–309, 378–380, 533–535, 618–622, 665–669, 988–989)

On July 7, 1937, a clash was provoked between Chinese and Japanese troops at the town of Lukouchiao. Hostilities followed. China appealed to the League on September 12, 1937, invoking Articles X, XI and XVII of the Covenant, but the Council merely referred the appeal to the Far Eastern Committee of the Assembly. This Committee adopted a resolution condemning the aerial bombardment of open towns by Japan. At this point, President Franklin D. Roosevelt

made his "Quarantine" Speech (October 5, 1937) which encouraged
the Committee to report that Japanese actions were "out of all pro-
portion to the incident that occasioned the conflict" and that Japan
had violated the Kellogg-Briand Pact and the Nine-Power Treaty.
The Assembly approved this report, advocated consultation among
the other signatories of the Nine-Power Pact and recommended that
all League powers refrain from any action weakening China and
consider means by which they could individually help China. The
Council passed a similar resolution, repeating it in February and
May of 1938.

In September, 1938, China appealed again for help. Japan having
declined to accept temporary membership under Article XVII, the
Council authorized and urged all Members to apply individual
sanctions under Article XVI. Another Council resolution to the
same effect was passed on May 27, 1939.

THE FINNISH-RUSSIAN CASE BEFORE THE COUNCIL OF THE LEAGUE OF NATIONS
(Articles XI and XV; Referred also to Assembly; Articles XII and XVI:
Official Journal, 1939, 496, 505–508, 509–542; *1940,* 11–23)

On December 3, 1939, the Finnish Government appealed to the
Secretary-General, by virtue of Articles XI and XV, to summon a
meeting of the Council and the Assembly so that necessary measures
might be taken to end the Soviet aggression which had started on
November 30.

The Secretary-General sent the letter to League Members on
December 3 and asked the Council to meet at Geneva on December
9. At the same time he asked the President of the Assembly to con-
voke the Assembly for December 11.

On December 9 the Council considered the appeal of the Finnish
Government. The representative of Finland, invoking Article XV,
paragraph 9, asked the Council to refer the dispute to the Assembly
without delay, which the Council did.

The Assembly began its session on December 11 and formed a
Special Committee to study the appeal (thirteen members). This
Committee attempted, under Article XV, to get the parties to the

dispute to cease hostilities and open negotiations under Assembly mediation. This offer was accepted by Finland only. In its Report, the Committee found that the Soviet had violated, not only its special political agreements with Finland, but also Article XII of the Covenant and the Pact of Paris. The Report was unanimously accepted by the Assembly, which in its Resolution recommended that the Council pronounce on the question under Article XVI. The Council met on December 14, 1939, and decided that in virtue of Article XVI, paragraph 4, the Soviet Government had placed itself outside the League of Nations and was no longer a Member thereof. Finland, Yugoslavia and China abstained from voting. There were no negative votes.

III

Manchuria and Ethiopia

1. THE MANCHURIAN INCIDENT

ON THE NIGHT of September 18, 1931, the Japanese Quantung Army, which was policing the South Manchurian Railway, alleged that there had been an explosion on the railway at Mukden and immediately seized the arsenal of the city and the strong points around it. Although the command of the Japanese forces was situated at Dairen on the coast over a hundred miles away, the garrison at Mukden had been carrying out maneuvers and before morning were in full possession of the ancient capital of Manchuria. The important cities of Ch'ang-ch'un and Kirin were also occupied within a few days. The Chinese claimed, and the subsequent evidence justifies the claim, that the coup had been planned beforehand by the Manchurian Command, although it was equally evident that the civilian branches of the Japanese Government, including the Foreign Office, had been kept in the dark by the militarists. The Japanese foreign policy was still under the control of the liberal party with Shidehara in the Foreign Office, although the Manchurian situation was extremely difficult. There was not only the rival effort of the Chinese to lessen the Japanese monopoly of the Manchurian Railway by building two other railway lines, but there was also banditry along the Japanese railway line, which called for extensive police measures and even then was never wholly overcome. The Mukden Incident of September 18 was the answer of the army to this situation. It was evident, however, that it constituted a threat of war, a threat with which the Chinese Government was ill-prepared to deal and which the Japanese Government naturally sought to minimize. Happily, the League of Nations had both Council and Assembly in session at the time, and it at once took cognizance of the Manchurian Incident.

Like the shot fired at Sarajevo seventeen years earlier, the shots fired in the railroad yards at Mukden constituted the overt act which led to war. But in both cases the real cause of the war lay in the subsequent failure of diplomacy to prevent the tragic consequences of that act in the breakdown of the structure of peace. In 1914 it was the state system of Europe, based on the balance of power, which, in the face of determined aggression, had no adequate means of self-defense. The first World War was largely due to the fact that in the hour of crisis there were only divided councils, especially as the aggression had been so definitely provoked. It was to prevent such confusion among the nations anxious for the preservation of peace that the League of Nations was established, with its provision for collective security. But in 1931, almost the same kind of confusion prevailed at Geneva as had been the case in the tragic days of August, 1914. This, however, was due not merely to the inadequacy of the machinery of the League of Nations, but also to the fact that the United States was not a member of it. With the best will in the world toward the League, Secretary Stimson found himself in the critical opening hours of the crisis more or less in the position of a rival to the League Council. This at least was the view taken by the Japanese who made much of any divergence of points of view between Washington and Geneva. The lesson from this failure to co-ordinate a power outside the League with the collective security which it was supposed to offer is obvious. The strategy of peace must be as direct and effective as that of war and this cannot be the case so long as there are separate directives, for the inevitable result of such confusion is either delay or inaction.

The first step taken by the League was to appeal to the governments of China and Japan "to refrain from any action which might aggravate the situation or prejudice the peaceful settlement of the problem" and to withdraw their troops immediately. This appeal communicated to Washington brought forth a cordial endorsement and the statement that it was working along the same lines. But two days later (September 23), when the Council began to consider favorably the appointment of a commission of inquiry to report on conditions in Manchuria, the Japanese Delegation in Geneva had word from Washington that Mr. Stimson was opposed to any such move and was critical of the Council's tactics. This was confirmed by the American representative at Geneva, who had been advised by telephone from Washington that it did not accept the thesis that the Peace Pact had been violated and was unwilling to take part in the commission. Here, at the very outset, we come upon what was perhaps the fatal blunder of the United States, for it checked the only positive action which the League could take at the time, an action which had proved effective when it prevented the outbreak of war between Greece and Bulgaria and one which ultimately, in the Lytton Commission, accomplished the only measure of constructive statesmanship that the peace forces were able to achieve in the Sino-Japanese dispute.

And yet Washington was not wholly to blame, for the spirit which animated Geneva at the time—especially in certain circles of the Secretariat—was so manifestly anti-Japanese that the proposal, fathered as it was by China, seemed more like the summoning of Japan as a guilty party than the erection of a purely impartial fact-finding body. Washington was misled by the hope that the militaristic elements in Japan would be held in check by the liberals still in charge of the Foreign Office and the Government in Tokyo, supported as they were by the commercial and business circles opposed to territorial expansion. The reminder by Mr. Stimson that the League's best ally might be found in Japan itself—for that is what his withdrawal amounted to—was certainly in keeping with the best traditions of diplomacy, but this need not have taken the shape of opposition to the appointment of a commission of investigation. As it was, the negative action of the United States played into the hands of Japan at Geneva, and the Council adjourned on September 30 for two weeks without taking any positive action. It merely requested both Japan and China to do all in their power to restore peace and asked that it be kept informed. This is what Japan had wanted.

Meanwhile, events in the Far East had shown Washington that the only hope for success lay in recovering the lost ground at Geneva, and on October 5 it sent a memorandum to the League, which seemed almost like giving it a blank check, that it would "reinforce what the League does." As the League had not done anything yet, this note seemed to the critics of the Administration to put the United States in a wholly wrong relation to the League because it implied a support for League policies in the shaping of which it would have no part. When the Council met on October 13, on a hint from Washington, Mr. Prentiss Gilbert, United States Consul at Geneva, was invited to sit at the Council table. For two whole days, Japan vigorously opposed this action, and there were many in the League itself who admitted the strength of its argument that the United States could not be both inside and outside the League even for the purpose of securing support for the Pact of Paris. Mr. Gilbert won this support, however, and all Members of the Council except China and Japan decided to join in an appeal to those Powers to respect the Pact; the notes were to be sent by each government separately so as to make easier the co-operation of the United States. Having secured this action, Washington might have been expected to join in it immediately, but two or three days passed before it followed up the diplomatic move of the other nations by a similar move of its own. Mr. Gilbert's consultation with the Council was rigorously limited, and it was obvious that the United States was again more busily employed in mollifying Japan than in the endeavor "to reinforce what the League does."

Left to itself, the Council drafted a resolution on October 24 which called upon the Japanese Government to withdraw its troops into the zone of the South Manchurian Railway "before the date fixed for the next meeting of the Council," which was November 16. This "ultimatum," as Japan regarded it, did not have the backing of the United States, and in the following days the Japanese army reached out on the south to seize the salt revenue at the seaport of Newchang and on the north to control important bridgeheads. M. Briand, as President of the Council, protested vigorously, but, although it ultimately supported the Council resolution except for the time limit, Washington was silent for two whole weeks as to whether it was going to support the Council's action or continue temporizing with

Japan. The uncertainty and confusion in which the League was left at this critical juncture was dramatized by the action of Ambassador Dawes on the occasion of the November Council meeting at Paris. Summoned from London, Mr. Dawes got as far as the Ritz Hotel on the north bank of the Seine, and during the very days that the Japanese generals were overrunning the whole of Manchuria, he remained in isolation while the Council was meeting at the Quai d'Orsay across the river, maintaining an informal liaison with it through Mr. Arthur Sweetser, the American member of the League Secretariat, who had also the full confidence of the Secretary-General. The situation was too serious to be comical, but it was manifestly absurd. Soon ugly rumors were afloat that the United States had made or was making secret agreements with Japan, and Secretary Stimson felt obliged to make a public statement that he had never promised Japan that the United States would not take part in an economic boycott or the withdrawal of ambassadors and that his government had "made no commitments, either expressed or implied, to either of the disputants." When a government is brought to the point where it deems it necessary to disclaim dishonorable action—for to have made secret terms with Japan after having given the League such an emphatic endorsement could not be regarded as honorable dealing—there is something very wrong in the situation in which it finds itself. No one with the slightest knowledge of American traditions, let alone acquaintance with the personalities at the State Department, could hold for a minute to the idea of an arrangement between the United States and Japan or any other Power under these or any other similar circumstances. But the fact cannot be passed by, in an appraisal of the strategy of peace in 1931, that unity of action, which was the only hope for success for either the United States or the League, was hopelessly far from attainment.

Strangely enough, it was Japan itself which, at this Paris meeting of the Council (December 10, 1931), brought up again the proposal for a commission of inquiry which it and the United States had refused to accept in the very first days of the dispute. This time we endorsed it in general but most cordial terms, and General Frank

McCoy became a member of the Lytton Commission of the League of Nations.

By the end of the year 1932, the Japanese occupation of South Manchuria was complete, the Chinese Government being unable to take any effective measures against it. With the Japanese forces on the borders of China itself, Secretary Stimson on January 7 sent identical notes to the governments of Japan and China setting forth the principle which became popularly known in the United States as the "Stimson Doctrine," that the United States "does not intend to recognize any situation or agreement which may be brought about by means contrary to the covenants and obligations of the Pact of Paris of August 27, 1928, to which treaty both China and Japan, as well as the United States, are parties."

Precedent for the "Stimson Doctrine" could be found in Latin-American history as far back as 1889 when the first International Conference of American States, meeting at Washington, passed a resolution to the effect that arbitration should be strengthened by acceptance of the principle that "conquest shall not, during the continuance of the treaty of arbitration, be recognized as admissible under American public law." This text was built upon by subsequent Conferences of the American States and formulated by the American Institute of International Law, chiefly under the inspiration of Dr. James Brown Scott. More pertinent to this history, however, is the fact that when Japan launched its twenty-one demands upon China, Secretary Bryan sent a dispatch to the hard-pressed government at Peking, applying the doctrine to maintain the territorial integrity of China. The "Stimson Doctrine" was, however, not backed by any willingness of the United States to enforce it. Senator Borah was still at the height of the influence which he had attained when in the drafting of the Kellogg-Briand Pact he prevented the inclusion of any measures of enforcement.

Unable to make headway militarily against the Japanese aggression, the Chinese undertook an intense boycott of Japanese goods. This was so successful that the Japanese landed seventy thousand troops at Shanghai and destroyed a section of that city.

The day after the Japanese landing at Shanghai, on January 29,

1932, the Chinese member of the Council of the League of Nations, convinced that the Council would not take effective action, invoked paragraph 9 of Article 15 of the Covenant, which provided that "The Council may in any case under this Article refer the dispute to the Assembly. The dispute shall be so referred at the request of either party to the dispute, provided that such request be made within 14 days after the submission of the dispute to the Council."

On February 12, the day on which the time limit would have expired, the Chinese Delegate, Dr. Yen, wrote to the Secretary-General that the Chinese Government was "constrained hereby to request that the [Sino-Japanese] dispute be referred to the Assembly." He added, however, that the Chinese Government would withdraw its request if the Council itself should decide to refer the dispute to the Assembly "in virtue of the general powers vested in it to summon the Assembly for consideration of the dispute."

The Committee of Twelve of the Council, to which the whole Manchurian matter was referred, considered this request in private meetings. The Japanese raised technical objections to the proposal which were referred to a Committee of Jurists. Keeping strictly to the legal points at issue, this Committee advised that as the Chinese request had not been withdrawn, the Council was bound to act upon it. Finally, on February 19, the Council adopted a Resolution referring the dispute to the Assembly and setting the meeting for March 3. Again the time table is interesting, because it was only the day before, on February 18, that the independence of Manchukuo (Manchuria) was proclaimed, and Henry P'Ui, the former Emperor of China, was installed as Regent. It should be noted that in the Resolution of the Council transferring the dispute to the Assembly, the Council reaffirmed its position under Article 11 of the Covenant, stating that its work for the maintenance of peace would continue unaffected by the fact that the Assembly was also dealing with the problem. The Japanese delegate did not oppose this resolution, but repeated the objections of the Japanese Government to the application of Article 15 to the Japanese-Chinese incident.

It is not possible to follow in detail the rest of this story, but it should be noted that the delays in the action of the League during the decisive winter of 1932 was partly due to the fact that the Great Powers were turned for the time being to direct diplomacy, which was equally futile. In May, China was obliged to sign an agreement establishing a demilitarized zone around the international settlement at Shanghai and to terminate the boycott. During the summer and autumn of 1932 the Lytton Commission of the League, which had been authorized at the Council meeting of December, 1931, visited Japan, Manchuria and China and reported to the Council in October. It stated that the Japanese action in Mukden was not in self-defense and that the creation of Manchukuo was not due to "any genuine and spontaneous independent movement," and recommended the establishment of an autonomous administration under Chinese sovereignty which would recognize Japanese economic interests and would have international advisors and police. In view of the fact that the Manchurian Episode had now been taken over by the Assembly, it was that body which approved the Stimson Report at the same time that it accepted the text of a Declaration which Mr. Stimson had made on August 8 which, in effect, tied in the Pact of Paris with Article 11 of the Covenant. For he stated that the Pact had changed the concept of neutrality by making a war anywhere "of concern to everybody connected with the Pact," and that consultation was necessarily implied in it. This was answered by Japan's recognition of Manchukuo.

Looking back over the history of the "Manchurian Incident," one can see the advantage which the Japanese militarists had because of the fact that they could make their plans in secret and carry them out regardless of any other national interest than that of Japan. The effort to check them suffered from an anarchy in command, due largely to the fact that the United States and the League did not work effectively together in the critical opening days and that later on it was extremely difficult, if not impossible, to recover the ground that had been lost. The possibilities of collective security were never fully explored because co-ordination of policy was lacking. In the absence of the United States and Russia from the League of Nations, there was no agreed method of consultation, and no very clear idea of what consultation meant.

But it would leave a false impression if the narrative were to stop short at this point without a criticism of the League's own failures. For if the Japanese tested the Pact of Paris, both by denying that it was violated when they took measures of self-defense in Manchuria and by refusing to admit the interest of co-signatories, they struck a still more serious blow at the League of Nations when they refused to admit its competence to intervene. It was not the Great Powers that felt this most, but small nations such as Switzerland, the Scandinavian States and Czechoslovakia, nations which looked to the League as the guaranty of their security and which, therefore, viewed with grave alarm any weakening of its authority. But the Great Powers pointed out that it would be they and not the smaller nations that would be called upon to enforce the sanctions of the Covenant if they should be invoked. In other words, the system which promised security to the smaller Powers seemed to threaten England and France with the insecurity that would follow from war in Asia. Great Britain had always shown reluctance to become the policeman of the League as the great sea Power whose interest touched so many distant lands. In this case it would not have to reckon with the possible hostility of the United States, intent upon maintaining its neutral rights if Britain were to enforce a League blockade against Japan; but commercial England was apparently uncertain how much its material interests in Asia might suffer if it started along the roadway of pacification cheered by the United States but found itself alone at the end of the road. France was keen for pacification but had not the slightest desire to undertake the task at cost to itself. Evidently the obligations of the Covenant called for more and greater sacrifices than the States that were members of the League were prepared to make. The Covenant had provided that there should be collective measures of peace enforcement but properly enough had not turned over to the League the control of the actual operation of those measures. To have done so would have been to create an international state with sovereign authority, which was the very thing which the makers of the Covenant tried to avoid. But this situation left the Member States still strongly conscious of the advantages of neutrality. Mr. Stimson's statement that the Pact of

Paris had ended the old freedom which allowed nations to remain
indifferent to the conflicts of others had been accepted as an academic
principle by all Members of the League of Nations. But now, when
suddenly passed from the field of academic discussion to that of
practical politics, it proved to be more than even the most ardent
pro-Leaguer was ready to carry out. In short, the Asiatic conflagra-
tion burst out in an unfinished edifice of international relations
which was still piled with the scaffolding of earlier days, and in
which the supporting buttresses—of co-operation and mutual assistance—were not yet wholly in place.

With both the British and the French reluctant, for different
reasons, to take strong measures against Japan, it was evident that
the Japanese had tested the structure of the League at a point of
fundamental weakness in the actual working out of collective security. It was clear that there never had been a full realization of
the extent to which the Great Powers might be involved if Article 11
of the Covenant were invoked, which stated that any war or threat
of war anywhere in the world was a matter of concern to all Members of the League, which "should take any action that may be
deemed wise and effectual to safeguard the peace of nations." The
test of this central obligation of the Covenant by a Great Power was
unfortunately made under the most adverse circumstances for the
League. It was an incident in a part of the world distant from Europe
and it happened at a time when the European nations were face to
face with grave economic and political crises at home. Both the
timing and the geographical situation of the military coup made it
almost inevitable that co-ordinated international action should be
difficult and that decisions for collective action would be delayed.
The Japanese militarists had evidently calculated their initial moves
with these factors in mind. The advantages of speed were on their
side. While their foreign office reiterated its professions of intention
to "localize the incident," in central Manchuria Kirin was occupied
on September 21 and the whole of Harbin in the north, by the 5th of
February, and it was not long before the whole of Manchuria was
overrun. Thus the situation played directly into the hands of the

Japanese militarists with the result that they were able, in the succeeding years, to seize and maintain the power which led them to attempt the conquest, not only of China, but—as they fondly dreamed—of all Asia.

2. THE ETHIOPIAN WAR

ETHIOPIA, bordered on north and south by Italian colonies, was a natural goal for Italian ambition. Admitted to the League in 1923 subject to certain conditions regarding slavery and arms traffic, the ancient kingdom had made undoubted progress under Haile Selassie I, but social revolutions are not made in a dozen years, and Ethiopia remained a backward state, lacking full control over tribes in frontier regions. Italy, still remembering her defeat by Ethiopian warriors in 1896 and feeling herself ill-treated in colonial matters by the other powers at Versailles, was faced with very real economic difficulties, for which she sought solution by gaining territories that would be sources of raw materials, that could be called outlets for surplus population, or that would provide the means of diverting attention from conditions at home.

The immediate cause of the dispute was a clash of Ethiopian and Italian native troops on December 5, 1934, at Wal Wal, an oasis near the long-disputed boundary between Ethiopia and Italian Somaliland. Under an Italo-Ethiopian treaty of 1928 the dispute was referred eventually to an arbitration commission. Italy subjected every step of the procedure to delay and obstinacy, and got from the League Council such an interpretation of the commission's duties that its effectiveness was considerably decreased. The proceedings dragged out for months, months in which Italy took full advantage to build up her military strength in East Africa, and finally on December 3 a decision was announced in which neither side was found guilty.

The matter had been called to the attention of the League in

December and again in January, 1935, and on March 17 Ethiopia
asked for Council action under Article 15 of the Covenant, not just
on the Wal Wal incident, but on the whole of the dangerous situation. The Council, preoccupied with other matters, preferred to
leave settlement in the hands of the parties and limited its activity
to assisting in arrangements for direct negotiations and arbitral procedure. Finally, on September 4 a general examination of the quar-
rel was undertaken, and on the same day Italy presented a long
memorandum citing repeated examples of Ethiopian aggression,
alleging default on the conditions of her entry into the League, and
denying the right of Ethiopia to equal status with Italy.

It is important to consider the attitudes of France and Great
Britain, since the two powers played an active part both during
direct negotiations and arbitration and a controlling part in League
action. France, in serious financial difficulties, was confronted also
with intense antagonisms between right and left which had gone to
the extreme of the formation of the so-called "armed leagues"; but
her major concern was with her security; and, faced with a re-arming
Germany, her sole recourse seemed to be to find allies. An important
step in this effort was the Franco-Italian pact of January 7, 1935.
These agreements, besides stating mutual concern over Austrian independence, made minor territorial readjustments in Africa and
certain economic concessions to Italy in Ethiopia; it seemed a victory
to secure an ally at such small cost. There were rumors of undis-
closed agreements; M. Laval firmly denied any understanding with
Mussolini as to Italian pressure on Ethiopia.[1] But if there were no
such understandings, the very existence of the pact, placed as it was
in an atmosphere of overwhelming fear of Germany, meant that
Mussolini could be fairly certain of touching a sensitive spot when
the necessity presented itself.

Across the Channel, events were moving differently. An excellent
opportunity to gauge British opinion was provided by the Peace Ballot, an unofficial poll sponsored by the League of Nations Union,

[1]E.g., in the Chamber of Deputies, December 28, 1935, *Journal Officiel,* December
29, 1935, p. 2865; Léon-Jean Cibot, *L'Éthiopie et la Société des Nations* (Paris,
1939), pp. 81–85.

results of which were announced on June 27, 1935. Representing the opinion of slightly less than 40 per cent of the total electorate of the United Kingdom, the voters showed themselves overwhelmingly in favor of remaining in the League and of reducing armaments, with nearly 90 per cent in favor of economic sanctions against an aggressor and almost 60 per cent fully in favor of military measures in such a case. Other expressions of British opinion indicated the same trend, notably in the instance of the resignation of the pacifist, George Lansbury, from the headship of the Labor Party. Inheritors of an opportunistic and pacifist foreign policy set forth by Sir John Simon, the government did not fail to take cognizance of these expressions. The change in government in 1935 made necessary a general election, held November 14, and preceded by a campaign in which collective security and loyalty to the League were the chief talking points. The great victory of the National Government could be interpreted as a mandate; on September 11 Sir Samuel Hoare, the Foreign Secretary, had pledged his country to full support of the Covenant in a speech before the Assembly. It remained to be seen how thoroughly the government would follow through that mandate.[2]

Neither the British nor the French were anxious to have the Ethiopian question come before the Council in January, but, faced with Ethiopian moderation and the contrary opinion of other members of the Council, they gave way and were instrumental in bringing Italy to do so. Their influence was asserted throughout the direct negotiations, particularly as the British became more and more apprehensive. But the predominant note was that of conciliation, of finding some sort of settlement which would not offend Italy, cause her to withdraw from the League, break the common front arrived at at Stresa in March, or undo the work of the pact of Rome of January. "Everything went on," remarked one commentator, "as if they wanted to allow Italy the delays necessary

[2]Arnold J. Toynbee, *Survey of International Affairs, 1935,* II, *Abyssinia and Italy* (London, 1935), pp. 38–70. Helen Hiett, *Public Opinion and the Italo-Ethiopian Dispute* (Geneva, 1936). Sir Samuel Hoare's speech, League of Nations *Official Journal, Special Supplement* (hereafter *O. J. S. S.*), No. 138 (1935), pp. 43–46.

methodically to prepare her expedition and to face the League with a *fait accompli*."[3]

⌐ Great Britain made a direct attempt at solution in June, when she offered to cede to Ethiopia a strip of British Somaliland with access to the sea, in compensation for territorial and economic concessions by Ethiopia to Italy. This effort encountered a firm Italian refusal, and the same fate met a suggestion of collective assistance to Ethiopia, recognizing special Italian interests, put forward by Great Britain and France during talks held in August among the three powers as signatories of a 1906 treaty concerning the integrity of Ethiopia.[4]

So it was again with the first attempt of the Council at action in the matter. On September 6 the Committee of Five—the United Kingdom, France, Poland, Turkey, and Spain—was appointed, and a plan was drawn up which was essentially a combination of the two offers previously made—a plan of international assistance to Ethiopia in carrying out the conditions of her entrance into the League, plus an announcement that territorial adjustments might be arranged in which Great Britain and France would be willing to sacrifice certain portions of their Somaliland territory as compensation to Ethiopia. It was also indicated that they would look with favor on economic agreements made between the two disputants, providing existing French and British interests were protected. The plan, presented to the two governments on September 18, was at once accepted by Ethiopia as a basis for negotiation, but Italy refused to have anything to do with the suggestions.[5] Under paragraph 4 of Article 15 of the Covenant, the Council appointed on September 26 a Committee of Thirteen to draft a report on the dispute, while the Committee of Five was to remain in existence, should opportunities for further attempts at conciliation appear.[6]

[3]G. Scelle, quoted in Cibot, *op. cit.*, p. 99.

[4]*Parliamentary Debates*, Commons, 5th series, CCCIII (1935–1936), pp. 1521–1522; League of Nations *Official Journal* (hereafter *O. J.*), November, 1935, pp. 1133–1135.

[5]*O. J.*, November, 1935, pp. 1145, 1204–1205, 1620–1627.

[6]This report, which reviews the whole history of the case before the League, is found in *O. J.*, November, 1935, pp. 1605–1619.

Meanwhile, the rainy season over, events in Africa moved rapidly. On October 3 Italy announced that Ethiopia had "succeeded in imposing" war on Italy and cited the Ethiopian mobilization order of September 28 in support of the Italian step in taking "the necessary measures of defence." An examination of these developments by a Committee of Six, set up on October 5, led to a report two days later which concluded that Italy had resorted to war "in disregard of its covenants under article 12 of the Covenant," and the findings were agreed to by all the members of the Council except Italy.[7]

The sixteenth ordinary session of the Assembly had opened on September 9 and by September 28 the work on the agenda had been accomplished. Several delegations had, however, approached the President or Secretary-General with a request that, in view of the tense situation, the meetings of the Assembly be adjourned rather than closed. The recommendation of the General Committee to this effect was adopted. M. Benes, President of the Assembly, kept in touch with the activity of the Council, with which he had declared the Assembly's decision was in no way to interfere, and on October 5 he decided that the situation warranted the reconvening of the Assembly in pursuance of the intention expressed on September 28. After noting that fourteen members of the Council had agreed to the report of the Committee of Six, the President of the Council at once announced that the Council "has now to assume its duty of co-ordination in regard to the measures to be taken. Since the Assembly of the League of Nations is convened for the day after tomorrow . . . my colleagues will doubtless feel it desirable to associate the Assembly with their task." The resolution and minutes of the meeting were forwarded to the President of the Assembly. M. Benes remarked in presenting them:

> The gravity of the fresh developments to which I have referred would seem to justify any emergency or other procedure, for the Assembly is entitled, under the actual provisions of the Covenant, to deal with any matter in the sphere of action of the League as affecting the peace of the world. Moreover, the Assembly is free to determine its own procedure and could regard the communica-

[7] *O. J.*, November, 1935, pp. 1217-1226, 1601-1605.

tion from the President of the Council as a report from the Council to the Assembly which has been officially referred to it.

He noted, however, that the matter remained before the Council and that the Assembly was neither replacing the Council nor reviewing the question of procedure followed by the Council under Article 15.[8] The Assembly, then, assumed a role in the co-ordination of sanctions which was neither absolutely necessary nor even expected in discussions of sanctions procedures in the early years of the League's existence. But the fact that the initiative had come from several delegations and the general acceptance which the plan received would seem to indicate that in 1935 the course was a natural one; moreover, there were excellent reasons for such co-operation. It had the advantage of associating with the action a greater number of States, especially those whose role might be important but who were not on the Council. Above all, it made for speed in a situation where each State Member was its own judge as to the existence of a violation of the Covenant. Italy, of course, Austria, Hungary, and later Albania dissented; the silence of other delegations was taken as implying consent.

Given the desire to associate all the participating States with the direction of the undertaking, and in view of the expense which would be involved in keeping the entire Assembly in session, it was decided to invite States Members, less the parties to the dispute, to send representatives to a Co-ordination Committee; the desire to avoid any obstruction on the part of Italy may have played a part in this decision as well. The somewhat equivocal constitutional position of this body—it was officially an organ neither of the Council nor of the Assembly, but a conference of Member States—was attacked by Italy, but without real effect on the issue. The first meeting was held on October 11, when for obvious reasons of efficency it was decided to set up a smaller operating committee, eventually to become the Committee of Eighteen; that Committee in turn organized a hierarchy of subcommittees.[9]

[8] *O. J.*, November, 1935, p. 1226; *O. J. S. S.*, No. 138 (1935), pp. 95, 98–100.

[9] Albert E. Highley, *The Actions of the States Members of the League of Nations in Application of Sanctions against Italy, 1935–1936* (Geneva, 1938), pp. 81–82, 86–94; *O. J. S. S.*, No. 138 (1935), pp. 109–114.

The first two of the Committee's recommendations to the governments may be disposed of without extended discussion. Proposal I, October 11, called for a lifting of any embargo on arms shipments to Ethiopia and for the imposition of such an embargo against Italy. Proposal II, October 14, extended to the suspension of financial, banking, and credit transactions with the offending State.[10] The next two proposals are of considerably greater importance and interest, and a somewhat more detailed examination will be worth while.

Proposals III and IV as finally drafted and adopted on October 19 involved an embargo on all imports from Italy to participating States and an embargo on certain items of export from those States to Italy—draft animals, rubber, and certain metals, including iron ore and scrap iron. The British thesis, as advanced by Mr. Eden in the Committee of Eighteen on October 12 stressed the necessity for speedy action and pointed out that the first of these measures, an embargo in imports, could readily be put into effect through existing machinery in almost all States, would avoid the problem of non-participating States, and would moreover be highly effective in that, by cutting off about 70 per cent of Italy's export trade, the means for executing purchases abroad would virtually disappear. Like Proposal II, its effect would be indirect. As to the embargo on exports, Mr. Eden maintained that time would be required to decide on categories to be included and to settle questions relating to the machinery for handling such an embargo.

The French representative considered, however, that the former question was quite as complicated as the latter and should be referred also to a technical subcommittee, a conclusion from which Mr. Eden strongly dissented. It seems apparent that the primary, though unexpressed, concern of the French Government was to delay both steps by reference to committee. The statement of M. Coulondre at this time is significant: "If a choice had to be made between the different possible measures, as France hoped that a pacific settlement might yet be reached, she would give her preference to the measures that were least irritating to the party to which

[10] *O. J. S. S.*, No. 145 (1936), pp. 14, 16.

they were to be applied. . . ." On October 14, however, Mr. Eden gave in to the French position, and both problems were referred to subcommittees. The date for coming into force of these two proposals was set later as November 18.[11]

The fifth recommendation of the Committee concerned the organization of mutual support, that is, of so diverting and rearranging trade among participating States as to compensate States, so far as possible, for losses due to the cutting off of exports to Italy, losses which might otherwise have serious economic and political repercussions. Although several schemes were debated, in the event the plan was to leave arrangements to negotiations among particular States on the lines of general principles laid down in the proposal.[12]

It must be remembered that throughout the year and a half that the problem was before the League, more than one means of treatment was in use at the same time; thus mediation by the two principal powers went on during the period of direct negotiation and arbitration; the resort to collective action after the beginning of hostilities was to mean no cessation, but rather a stepping-up, of conciliatory efforts. Consideration must always be given to the state of public opinion both in France and England; some attempt must now be made at assessing the attitude of the responsible leaders of those two governments.

Mr. Baldwin had said in 1934: "If you are going to adopt a sanction, you must be prepared for war. If you adopt a sanction without being ready for war, you are not an honest trustee of the nation."[13] Elevated to the premiership, Mr. Baldwin still held to that premise, but as part of a paradoxical policy which Winston Churchill has summed up neatly:

The Prime Minister had declared that Sanctions meant war; secondly, he was resolved there must be no war; and thirdly, he decided upon Sanctions. It was evidently impossible to reconcile

---

[11]*O. J. S. S.*, No. 145 (1936), pp. 36–43, 56–57; on the French attitude, Highley, *op. cit.*, pp. 112–114.

[12]A clear discussion of this problem and the League's action is found in Highley, *op. cit.*, pp. 118–128, 226.

[13]*Parliamentary Debates*, Commons, 5th series, CCLXIX (1935–1936), p. 2139.

these three conditions. Under the guidance of Britain and the pressure of Laval, the League of Nations kept clear of any that would provoke war.[14]

About September 10 Sir Samuel Hoare and Pierre Laval decided that no military sanctions, no sanctions leading to the possibility of war would be adopted, should Italy disregard her obligations under the Covenant; be it noted that this is at the same time that Sir Samuel made his obeisance before the Assembly to the manifestation of British opinion in the Peace Ballot. Although this meeting was not disclosed until the end of the year, the decision was apparent throughout the period, notably in a speech given by M. Laval at Clermont-Ferrand, October 12, and in a statement by Sir Samuel in Commons, October 22.[15] The effect of this decision is perhaps decisive as a factor in the defeat of sanctions and the victory of appeasement.

Mention has already been made of a divergence between French and British approaches to the problem of sanctions, despite fundamental agreement on the matter just discussed. British fear of isolated action was great; even Winston Churchill recommended going no farther than France could be carried, which he thought was not very far.[16] But a forward public opinion pulled reluctant ministers after it; in discussions of sanctions the British representative played always an advanced role. Perhaps even more significant was the reinforcement of the Mediterranean fleet in September. Shortly thereafter, diplomatic correspondence between Great Britain and France took place, in which Britain sought assurances that, in case of attack on her by Italy as a result of action under Article 16, France would come to her aid; these assurances were given, and the question extended to, and favorable replies were received from, other Mediterranean powers.[17]

[14]*The Gathering Storm* (New York, 1948), p. 175.

[15]Laval in the Chamber of Deputies, December 28, 1935, *Journal Officiel,* December 29, 1935, p. 2863; excerpts from the Clermont-Ferrand speech can be found in *Documents on International Affairs, 1935* (London, 1937), II, p. 316; *Parliamentary Debates,* Commons, 5th Series, CCCV, p. 30.

[16]Churchill, *op. cit.,* p. 169.

[17]*Documents, 1935,* II, pp. 299, 304–313.

It is against this background of significant divergences and more significant agreements that the climax of the development must be seen. It will have been noticed that the embargo on exports to Italy was limited to a relatively restricted list of commodities; the French delegate had submitted two lists, the key to classification being the degree of control which States Members of the League exercised over those commodities. In the first list were included items such as finally appeared in Proposal IV, in which Italy was deficient and of which participating States were her principal suppliers. List two included the all-important coal, petroleum, copper, and finished or semifinished iron products. It has been suggested by one member of the Committee that this list was presented following telephone conversations between M. Laval and Mussolini, and he remarks that, in view of the position of France as an exporter of iron and steel and of Italy as dependent on imported coal and oil, the classification has a highly suspicious cast.[18] The distinction was not well received by countries producing raw material, for example, Spain and Canada. The Spanish member of the Committee in particular objected to the restrictions placed on the export of iron ore and scrap from his country, while manufacturing countries were in no way restricted in their shipment to Italy of processed iron and steel. It was clear also that the measures contemplated by Proposal IV left untouched the commodities, lack of which could quickly bring Italy to her knees; the Italians had imposed counter-embargoes on sanctionist countries, and had undertaken a stern program of domestic retrenchment and sacrifice to defeat the effect of sanctions; the prospect of their being extended to vital products was serious, and full expression was given to Italian views that such extension would be considered hostile.

On November 2 the Committee of Eighteen met. It was evident that sentiment for the extension of the embargo was growing, and a French proposal for extending it to oil, iron and steel, coal, and copper had been prepared, which, though approved by the officials of the Foreign Office, was not to be presented because of exception

[18] *O. J. S. S.*, No. 145 (1936), p. 87; W. A. Riddell, *World Security by Conference* (Toronto, [c] 1948), p. 109.

taken by M. Laval. The initiative was instead taken by Dr. Riddell, the Canadian representative, although he lacked any positive instructions from his government. As finally drafted and adopted on November 6, Proposal IVa called for an extension of Proposal IV to petroleum and its derivatives, pig-iron, iron and steel, coal, coke, and fuels derived from them. It should be noted that, in concession to the fact that the League did not exercise full control over these commodities, the proposal looked to an effective date "as soon as it appears that the acceptance of this principle is sufficiently general to ensure the efficacy of the measure thus contemplated. . . ."[19]

The extension of sanctions then was to a considerable degree rendered problematical by the existence of large producers of the commodities in question outside the League; of these the principal was the United States. The nonuniversality of the League was an argument reverted to again and again by Mr. Baldwin; a brief examination of the problem would therefore seem in order. The United States, although one of the two largest exporters of oil, provided only 6.6 per cent of Italy's needs from 1931 to 1934.[20] A very large increase had occurred during 1935, despite the opposition of the administration to such a development. Under the neutrality resolution of August 31, 1935 the President had invoked an arms embargo on October 5, but he was provided no other discretionary powers; the only tool left the administration was moral suasion, and this was used positively by the President, the Secretary of State, especially in his remarks of November 15, and by the Secretary of the Interior, who called on the petroleum industry to cease shipments to Italy. The ineffectiveness of these appeals, and doubt that the President's powers would be increased as a small but vocal section of American opinion was demanding, certainly had effect on the events unfolding in Europe, particularly in an England committed to a policy of close friendship with the United States. Professor Toynbee points out, however, that the indecisiveness of European action, particularly the Hoare-Laval pact, was in turn a deterrent to American action. In the neutrality legislation debate in 1936 a provision which gave the

[19] *O. J. S. S.*, No. 146 (1936), pp. 37–38, 46–47; Riddell, *op. cit.*, pp. 113–126.
[20] *O. J. S. S.*, No. 148 (1936), p. 72.

President wide discretionary powers over war material was eventually struck out, although an embargo on financial transactions was included.[21]

It has been noted that the Canadian delegate to the Committee undertook his significant move without specific authorization from his government. The news of his action reached Ottawa when the Department of External Affairs was in the hands of a French-Canadian Acting Minister; French-Canadian sentiment, strongly isolationist in any event, was affected by Italian propaganda, and it is probable that it was the action of Mr. Lapointe, later, to be sure, underwritten by the Prime Minister, which led to the disavowal of the Canadian delegate's action on December 1, a development which pleased Italy greatly, and which, although counteracted to a considerable degree by the unanimity with which the proposal had been received, was something of a blow to a united front in Geneva.[22]

The major consideration is the action of the French Government to which the United Kingdom was soon attached. It has been shown that the extension of sanctions was not at all in accord with the desires of the French Prime Minister. On the same day that Riddell had proposed the extension, Hoare and Laval announced to the Co-ordination Committee that they were still considering other methods than coercive and reasserted that any action would be taken through the League; in this announcement they were supported by other members of the Committee, led by Van Zeeland of Belgium; this "commission" was continually referred to in defense of the Anglo-French course.[23]

On November 22 it was announced that the Committee of Eighteen was to be called for the 29th to consider setting a date for the coming into force of the new sanctions. Laval requested, and got, a postponement of the meeting, ostensibly because of the pressure of parliamentary business, perhaps more truly because of

---

[21]On the situation in the United States, see Toynbee, *op. cit.,* pp. 239–248, and *Documents, 1935,* II, pp. 263–296.

[22]Riddell, *op. cit.,* pp. 127–136.

[23]*O. J. S. S.,* No. 146 (1936), pp. 8–9. Toynbee suggests that Van Zeeland's support was arranged beforehand, *op. cit.,* pp. 285–286.

Italian threats that carrying through the oil sanction would have repercussions in Italo-French relations. Italian announcements of certain unspecified military movements and rumors of retaliation against Britain added to the tenseness of the situation, and at Laval's request, with British assent, the postponed meeting was set for December 12. Italy then began conciliatory moves; assurance was given that no troop movements in the vicinity of the French frontier were planned, and it was stated that the oil sanction would be considered an unfriendly, but not a hostile, act. Meanwhile negotiations had been going on in Paris between Mr. Peterson for the Foreign Office and M. de St. Quentin of the Quai d'Orsay: their plan was completed early in December and served as the basis for the Hoare-Laval proposals.

On December 7 Sir Samuel Hoare made his trip to Paris. It has been claimed that the assertion that he stopped in Paris only incidentally to his vacation trip to Switzerland was "political camouflage."[24] In this regard, two points can be maintained with certainty; one, that the British Government could not have been taken quite so much by surprise, as was maintained in the sequel, by the proposals because of the preliminary negotiations which had been carried on with the full knowledge of the British Government: the other, that Sir Samuel was in definitely poor health, a fact which may have contributed to his susceptibility to the arguments of M. Laval. At any rate, Sir Samuel, already convinced of the futility of dependence on America, certain of Ethiopian defeat, and strongly advised that the oil sanction meant war, was further convinced by M. Laval, who apparently underlined the last conviction and implied that in event of an attack on the British fleet, French naval forces could not be brought into action for two weeks. Professor Toynbee believes that M. Laval was prepared to go even farther and to refuse French support altogether. The upshot of the conference was the Hoare-Laval plan, which called for the outright cession of certain Ethiopian territories to Italy, the granting of a much larger zone, still under nominal Ethiopian sovereignty, to Italy for exploitation and settlement, and the setting up of a scheme of international super-

[24]Riddell, *op. cit.,* p. 136.

vision for the rest of the country in which Italy would predominate. News of the decision leaked out in the Paris newspapers on December 9; on the 10th the decision of the British Cabinet to back the proposals was announced; and the offer was despatched to the two belligerents.[25]

The outcome may be briefly noted. Neither Italy nor Ethiopia accepted the plan. More interesting is the violent reaction of British public opinion; various organizational representations were reinforced by a great outburst of letters of protest. The Cabinet was forced to back down, saving itself at the price of Sir Samuel Hoare's resignation, and a tremendous loss in prestige. On December 19 Sir Samuel delivered an apologia in the House of Commons in which he made three principal points: that the oil sanction would have meant war, that he was oppressed by the fear that Ethiopia might be led to expect too much from the League, and that the British had got themselves into an untenable military position, unsupported by similar action on the part of any other country. In France, a strong reaction was provoked on the left, but the country at large was less aroused, and M. Laval was sustained by a fairly narrow margin to be sure, in a vote of confidence.[26] December 18 saw the withdrawal of British support before the League Council, and the next day the Council offered its thanks to the negotiators and turned the problem back to the Committee of Thirteen.[27]

The denouement may be rapidly surveyed. Although the affair lasted for another six months, the proceedings are as drab as they are tragic, and the whole is subordinate in importance to the new threat posed by the reoccupation of the Rhineland on March 7, 1936.

The question of the imposition of the extended sanctions had been postponed in view of the Hoare-Laval plan. The report of a com-

[25]Toynbee, *op. cit.*, pp. 277–305; Riddell, *op. cit.*, pp. 136–139: Vera M. Dean, *The Quest for Ethiopian Peace* (Geneva 1936). The texts of the communications embodying the plan may be found in Cmd. 5044, House of Commons, *Parliamentary Papers*, 1935–1936, XVII, p. 635, or in *Documents, 1935*, II, pp. 357–362.

[26]Hiett, *op. cit.*, pp. 21, 22; *Parliamentary Debates*, Commons, 5th series, CCCVII, pp. 2007–2017; *Journal Officiel*, December 29, 1935, p. 2868.

[27]*O. J.*, January, 1936, pp. 7–11

mittee of experts, appointed January 22, 1936, on the operation of an
oil embargo was made on February 12; on March 2 Mr. Eden
announced in the Committee of Eighteen that the British Government would support the imposition of an oil sanction. That the accusations made by Léon Blum that M. Laval's policy had been a
purely personal one were not entirely accurate is indicated by the
fact that M. Flandin, who had succeeded M. Laval at the Quai
d'Orsay on January 22, followed the same lead. He intervened on
March 3 to ask that the Committee of Thirteen make another
attempt at conciliation; appeals were promptly despatched, and
acceptances in principle were received during the month from both
belligerents. After exchanges of accusations of violations of the laws
of war, the parties failed to agree, and the fact was duly noted by
the Council, now preoccupied with other matters, on April 20.
Throughout the period the Ethiopian Government issued pleas for
additional sanctions and for financial aid, both to the League and
to the world at large, but they came to nothing. The campaign in
Ethiopia after a period of stagnation had suddenly in February
turned into a rout. On May 1 the Emperor left his capital which
was occupied by Italian troops four days later, and on May 9 Ethiopia
was declared under Italian sovereignty. With the war over and the
failure of the League in this instance manifest, there remained little
to do but to write a conclusion by the lifting of sanctions which no
longer had any excuse for existing; this was done, with only South
Africa dissenting, on July 6, to take effect on the 15th of the same
month.

That the great experiment failed should not obscure the fact that
sanctions, imperfectly though they were applied, were effective. Imports during the period of sanctions from Italy to participating
countries hovered at about half of the figures obtaining in the
previous year; the decline in exports to Italy was not so great, although by April of 1936 the figure had fallen very nearly to half.[28]
The stringent measures taken in Italy, the statements of the head of
the fascist state and of the Fascist Grand Council testify to their

[28]*Documents, 1935,* II, p. 243

power; even more eloquent was the real concern in Italy lest sanctions be extended.

But to some degree sanctions cut both ways. Albania, Austria, and Hungary refused to participate; but certain countries, especially in the Balkans, which did participate, considering their security of more importance then economic loss, suffered heavily. For example, one fifth of Yugoslavia's trade was with Italy, and, while Great Britain made a concession to mutual support by relaxing controls on certain Yugoslav products, that country found herself in a very difficult situation. Granted that the problem was one of great complexity, and that there existed no previous experience in its solution and no machinery to use, still it must be said that the failure to implement fully the provisions for mutual support in the economic field, by leading to a demand for exemptions, destroyed some of the effectiveness a solid front would have created and resulted in serious inequities.[29]

On the whole, however, the co-operation, given an enterprise without precedent, was satisfactory. Administrative and technical matters were well handled.[30]

It has been indicated that a much-used argument was and is that the failure was in large part due to the nonuniversal character of the League, with particular reference to the absence of the United States. That such a gap was very important there is no denying; it is, of course, impossible to say what course the government of the United States, faced with an overwhelming isolationist opinion, would have taken with respect to abnormal exports to Italy, had a thorough-going program of sanctions been adopted. That question mark loomed large in British thinking. But it would seem that this concern about the absence of certain large States was sometimes used as an excuse to blanket less commendable excuses.

One vital testimony of the failure of the program is to the need for speed; delayed at every juncture for political reasons, proceedings

---

[29]Toynbee, *op. cit.*, pp. 434–435.

[30]For opinions on these points based on detailed studies, see E. L. Léroux, *Le Conflit italo-ethiopien devant la S.D.N.* (Paris, 1937); R. A. Levitch, *La collaboration dans l'application des sanctions* (Paris, 1938); and Highley, *op. cit.*

within the League gave Italy every opportunity to plan and carry out her campaign, and a campaign once started is difficult to stop. In the case of oil, the committee of experts indicated that Italy had probably accumulated no abnormally large stocks of oil during 1934 and 1935, and that even in January, 1936, the imposition of an embargo would have found her with only three to three and a half months' supply on hand.[31] The effect of a sincere and uncompromising boycott in this field alone is easy to imagine.

The chief architect of the collapse of sanctions was, beyond a doubt, M. Laval. Building on a bitterly divided public opinion in his own country and playing upon the fears and hesitations of other leaders, he constructed a fantastic and terrible diplomacy. The whole story of his maneuverings is perhaps a perpetual secret, and the importance of his fascist sympathies, later so cruelly evident, in this instance cannot yet be properly assessed.

But the blame is not entirely his. The British Government had behind it a powerful bloc of public opinion, and without doubt public opinion would have rallied completely had Britain been attacked in the course of action in upholding the Covenant. Yet it was a Britain without sufficient arms. It can be seen now that the British fleet could have won any engagement against the Italians,[32] but British leaders were too timid to take the risk. It must be noted also that other powers seconded the conciliatory efforts of the two major powers at every step.

It was suggested above that the defeat of the extension of sanctions and the Hoare-Laval plan flowed from the decision against the use of military sanctions or of any sanction which might lead to war. French opinion on the whole called for peace at any price; for that Laval, if for different reasons, worked. In Britain, pacifism was still strong. The combination of conciliatory techniques with coercive measures can be successful only if there is evident a strong will to back up the latter if necessary. Had the willingness to use military force as a last resort in support of the Covenant been evident to Italy, its use might have been unnecessary, and the lesson would

[31]*O. J. S. S.,* No. 148 (1936), p. 67.

[32]This is Churchill's opinion, *The Gathering Storm,* pp. 176-177.

not have been lost on an interested observer to the north; had resort to it proved necessary, it might have been the means of preventing a more terrible war.[33]

[33]Other useful sources for this period are: Keith Feiling, *The Life of Neville Chamberlain* (London, 1946); Herbert Feis, *Seen from E. A.: Three International Episodes* (New York, 1947); Cordell Hull, *The Memoirs of Cordell Hull* (New York, 1948); *International Sanctions, a Report by a Group of Members of the Royal Institute of International Affairs* (London, 1938); A. de G. de la Pradelle, "Le Conflit italo-ethiopien," *Revue de Droit International*, XVI (1935); Pitman B. Potter, *The Wal Wal Arbitration* (Washington, 1938); John H. Spencer, "The Italian-Ethiopian Dispute and the League of Nations," *American Journal of International Law*, XXXI (1937), pp. 614–641.

Appendix

RESOLUTION XIV OF THE THIRD ASSEMBLY

1. No scheme for the reduction of armaments, within the meaning of Article 8 of the Covenant, can be fully successful unless it is general.

2. In the present state of the world many Governments would be unable to accept the responsibility for a serious reduction of armaments unless they received in exchange a satisfactory guarantee of the safety of their country.

3. Such a guarantee can be found in a defensive agreement which should be open to all countries, binding them to provide immediate and effective assistance in accordance with a pre-arranged plan in the event of one of them being attacked, provided that the obligation to render assistance to a country attacked shall be limited in principle to those countries situated in the same part of the globe. In cases, however, where, for historical, geographical, or other reasons, a country is in special danger of attack, detailed arrangements should be made for its defence in accordance with the above-mentioned plan.

4. As a general reduction of armaments is the object of the three preceding statements, and the Treaty of Mutual Guarantee the means of achieving that object, previous consent to this reduction is therefore the first condition of the Treaty.

This reduction could be carried out either by means of a general treaty, which is the most desirable plan, or by means of partial treaties designed to be extended and open to all countries.

In the former case, the Treaty will carry with it a general reduction of armaments. In the latter case, the reduction should be proportionate to the guarantees afforded by the Treaty.

The Council of the League, after having taken the advice of the Temporary Mixed Commission, which will examine how each of these two systems could be carried out, should further formulate and submit to the Governments for their consideration and sovereign decision the plan of the machinery, both political and military, necessary to bring them clearly into effect.[1]

[1]League of Nations, *Records of the Third Assembly, Plenary Meetings,* Text of the Debates, I, p. 291.

PROTOCOL FOR THE PACIFIC SETTLEMENT
OF INTERNATIONAL DISPUTES (1924)

Animated by the firm desire to ensure the maintenance of general peace and the security of nations whose existence, independence or territories may be threatened;

Recognising the solidarity of the members of the international community;

Asserting that a war of aggression constitutes a violation of this solidarity and an international crime;

Desirous of facilitating the complete application of the system provided in the Covenant of the League of Nations for the pacific settlement of disputes between States and of ensuring the repression of international crimes; and

For the purpose of realising, as contemplated by Article 8 of the Covenant, the reduction of national armaments to the lowest point consistent with national safety and the enforcement by common action of international obligations;

The undersigned, duly authorised to that effect, agree as follows:

ARTICLE I

The signatory States undertake to make every effort in their power to secure the introduction into the Covenant of amendments on the lines of the provisions contained in the following articles.

They agree that, as between themselves, these provisions shall be binding as from the coming into force of the present Protocol and that, so far as they are concerned, the Assembly and the Council of the League of Nations shall thenceforth have power to exercise all the rights and perform all the duties conferred upon them by the Protocol.

ARTICLE 2

The signatory States agree in no case to resort to war either with one another or against a State which, if the occasion arises, accepts all the obligations hereinafter set out, except in case of resistance to acts of aggression or when acting in agreement with the Council or the Assembly of the League of Nations in accordance with the provisions of the Covenant and of the present Protocol.

ARTICLE 3

The signatory States undertake to recognise as compulsory, ipso facto and without special agreement, the jurisdiction of the Permanent Court of International Justice in the cases covered by paragraph 2 of Article 36 of the Statute of the Court, but without prejudice to the right of any State, when acceding to the special protocol provided for in the said Article and opened for signature on December 16th, 1920, to make reservations compatible with the said clause.

Accession to this special protocol, opened for signature on December 16th, 1920, must be given within the month following the coming into force of the present Protocol.

States which accede to the present Protocol, after its coming into force, must carry out the above obligation within the month following their accession.

ARTICLE 4

With a view to render more complete the provisions of paragraphs 4, 5, 6 and 7 of Article 15 of the Covenant, the signatory States agree to comply with the following procedure:

1. If the dispute submitted to the Council is not settled by it as provided in paragraph 3 of the said Article 15, the Council shall endeavour to persuade the parties to submit the dispute to judicial settlement or arbitration.

2. (a) If the parties cannot agree to do so, there shall, at the request of at least one of the parties, be constituted a Committee of Arbitrators. The Committee shall so far as possible be constituted by agreement between the parties.

(b) If within the period fixed by the Council the parties have failed to agree, in whole or in part, upon the number, the names and the powers of the arbitrators and upon the procedure, the Council shall settle the points remaining in suspense. It shall with the utmost possible despatch select in consultation with the parties the arbitrators and their President from among persons who by their nationality, their personal character and their experience, appear to it to furnish the highest guarantees of competence and impartiality.

(c) After the claims of the parties have been formulated the Committee of Arbitrators, on the request of any party, shall through the medium of the Council request an advisory opinion upon any points of law in dispute from the Permanent Court of International Justice, which in such case shall meet with the utmost possible despatch.

3. If none of the parties asks for arbitration, the Council shall again take the dispute under consideration. If the Council reaches a report which is unanimously agreed to by the members thereof other than the representatives of any of the parties to the dispute, the signatory States agree to comply with the recommendations therein.

4. If the Council fails to reach a report which is concurred in by all its members, other than the representatives of any of the parties to the dispute, it shall submit the dispute to arbitration. It shall itself determine the composition, the powers and the procedure of the Committee of Arbitrators and, in the choice of the arbitrators, shall bear in mind the guarantees of competence and impartiality referred to in paragraph 2 (b) above.

5. In no case may a solution, upon which there has already been a unanimous recommendation of the Council accepted by one of the parties concerned, be again called in question.

6. The signatory States undertake that they will carry out in full good faith any judicial sentence or arbitral award that may be rendered and that they will comply, as provided in paragraph 3 above, with the solutions recommended by the Council. In the event of a State failing to carry out the above undertakings, the Council shall exert all its influence to secure compliance therewith. If it fails therein, it shall propose what steps should be taken to give effect thereto, in accordance with the provision contained

at the end of Article 13 of the Covenant. Should a State in disregard of the above undertakings resort to war, the sanctions provided for by Article 16 of the Covenant, interpreted in the manner indicated in the present Protocol, shall immediately become applicable to it.

7. The provisions of the present Article do not apply to the settlement of disputes which arise as the result of measures of war taken by one or more signatory States in agreement with the Council or the Assembly.

ARTICLE 5

The provisions of paragraph 8 of Article 15 of the Covenant shall continue to apply in proceedings before the Council.

If in the course of an arbitration, such as is contemplated by Article 4 above, one of the parties claims that the dispute, or part thereof, arises out of a matter which by international law is solely within the domestic jurisdiction of that party, the arbitrators shall on this point take the advice of the Permanent Court of International Justice through the medium of the Council. The opinion of the Court shall be binding upon the arbitrators, who, if the opinion is affirmative, shall confine themselves to so declaring in their award.

If the question is held by the Court or by the Council to be a matter solely within the domestic jurisdiction of the State, this decision shall not prevent consideration of the situation by the Council or by the Assembly under Article 11 of the Covenant.

ARTICLE 6

If in accordance with paragraph 9 of Article 15 of the Covenant a dispute is referred to the Assembly, that body shall have for the settlement of the dispute all the powers conferred upon the Council as to endeavouring to reconcile the parties in the manner laid down in paragraphs 1, 2 and 3 of Article 15 of the Covenant and in paragraph 1 of Article 4 above.

Should the Assembly fail to achieve an amicable settlement:

If one of the parties asks for arbitration, the Council shall proceed to constitute the Committee of Arbitrators in the manner provided in subparagraphs (a), (b) and (c) of paragraph 2 of Article 4 above.

If no party asks for arbitration, the Assembly shall again take the dispute under consideration and shall have in this connection the same powers as the Council. Recommendations embodied in a report of the Assembly, provided that it secures the measure of support stipulated at the end of paragraph 10 of Article 15 of the Covenant, shall have the same value and effect, as regards all matters dealt with in the present Protocol, as recommendations embodied in a report of the Council adopted as provided in paragraph 3 of Article 4 above.

If the necessary majority cannot be obtained, the dispute shall be submitted to arbitration and the Council shall determine the composition, the powers and the procedure of the Committee of Arbitrators as laid down in paragraph 4 of Article 4.

ARTICLE 7

In the event of a dispute arising between two or more signatory States, these States agree that they will not, either before the dispute is submitted to proceedings for pacific settlement or during such proceedings, make any increase of their armaments or effectives which might modify the position established by the Conference for the Reduction of Armaments provided for by Article 17 of the present Protocol, nor will they take any measure of military, naval, air, industrial or economic mobilisation, nor, in general, any action of a nature likely to extend the dispute or render it more acute.

It shall be the duty of the Council, in accordance with the provisions of Article 11 of the Covenant, to take under consideration any complaint as to infraction of the above undertakings which is made to it by one or more of the States parties to the dispute. Should the Council be of opinion that the complaint requires investigation, it shall, if it deems it expedient, arrange for enquiries and investigations in one or more of the countries concerned. Such enquiries and investigations shall be carried out with the utmost possible despatch and the signatory States undertake to afford every facility for carrying them out.

The sole object of measures taken by the Council as above provided is to facilitate the pacific settlement of disputes and they shall in no way prejudge the actual settlement.

If the result of such enquiries and investigations is to establish an infraction of the provisions of the first paragraph of the present Article, it shall be the duty of the Council to summon the State or States guilty of the infraction to put an end thereto. Should the State or States in question fail to comply with such summons, the Council shall declare them to be guilty of a violation of the Covenant or of the present Protocol, and shall decide upon the measures to be taken with a view to end as soon as possible a situation of a nature to threaten the peace of the world.

For the purposes of the present Article decisions of the Council may be taken by two-thirds majority.

ARTICLE 8

The signatory States undertake to abstain from any act which might constitute a threat of aggression against another State.

If one of the signatory States is of opinion that another State is making preparations for war, it shall have the right to bring the matter to the notice of the Council.

The Council, if it ascertains that the facts are as alleged, shall proceed as provided in paragraphs 2, 4 and 5 of Article 7.

ARTICLE 9

The existence of demilitarised zones being calculated to prevent aggression and to facilitate a definite finding of the nature provided for in Article 10 below, the establishment of such zones between States mutually consenting thereto is recommended as a means of avoiding violations of the present Protocol.

The demilitarised zones already existing under the terms of certain treaties or conventions, or which may be established in future between States mutually consenting thereto, may at the request and at the expense of one or more of the conterminous States, be placed under a temporary or permanent system of supervision to be organised by the Council.

ARTICLE 10

Every State which resorts to war in violation of the undertakings contained in the Covenant or in the present Protocol is an aggressor. Violations of the rules laid down for a demilitarised zone shall be held equivalent to resort to war.

In the event of hostilities having broken out, any State shall be presumed to be an aggressor, unless a decision of the Council, which must be taken unanimously, shall otherwise declare:

1. If it has refused to submit the dispute to the procedure of pacific settlement provided by Articles 13 and 15 of the Covenant as amplified by the present Protocol, or to comply with a judicial sentence or arbitral award or with a unanimous recommendation of the Council, or has disregarded a unanimous report of the Council, a judicial sentence or an arbitral award recognising that the dispute between it and the other belligerent State arises out of a matter which by international law is solely within the domestic jurisdiction of the latter State; nevertheless, in the last case the State shall only be presumed to be an aggressor if it has not previously submitted the question to the Council or the Assembly, in accordance with Article 11 of the Covenant.

2. If it has violated provisional measures enjoined by the Council for the period while the proceedings are in progress as contemplated by Article 7 of the present Protocol.

Apart from the cases dealt with in paragraphs 1 and 2 of the present Article, if the Council does not at once succeed in determining the aggressor, it shall be bound to enjoin upon the belligerents an armistice, and shall fix the terms, acting, if need be, by a two-thirds majority and shall supervise its execution.

Any belligerent which has refused to accept the armistice or has violated its terms shall be deemed an aggressor.

The Council shall call upon the signatory States to apply forthwith against the aggressor the sanctions provided by Article 11 of the present Protocol, and any signatory State thus called upon shall thereupon be entitled to exercise the rights of a belligerent.

ARTICLE 11

As soon as the Council has called upon the signatory States to apply sanctions, as provided in the last paragraph of Article 10 of the present Protocol, the obligations of the said States, in regard to the sanctions of all kinds mentioned in paragraphs 1 and 2 of Article 16 of the Covenant, will immediately become operative in order that such sanctions may forthwith be employed against the aggressor.

Those obligations shall be interpreted as obliging each of the signatory States to co-operate loyally and effectively in support of the Covenant of the League of Nations, and in resistance to any act of aggression, in the degree which its geographical position and its particular situation as regards armaments allow.

In accordance with paragraph 3 of Article 16 of the Covenant the signatory States give a joint and several undertaking to come to the assistance of the State attacked or threatened, and to give each other mutual support by means of facilities and reciprocal exchanges as regards the provision of raw materials and supplies of every kind, openings of credits, transport and transit, and for this purpose to take all measures in their power to preserve the safety of communications by land and by sea of the attacked or threatened State.

If both parties to the dispute are aggressors within the meaning of Article 10, the economic and financial sanctions shall be applied to both of them.

ARTICLE 12

In view of the complexity of the conditions in which the Council may be called upon to exercise the functions mentioned in Article 11 of the present Protocol concerning economic and financial sanctions, and in order to determine more exactly the guarantees afforded by the present Protocol to the signatory States, the Council shall forthwith invite the economic and financial organisations of the League of Nations to consider and report as to the nature of the steps to be taken to give effect to the financial and economic sanctions and measures of co-operation contemplated in Article 16 of the Covenant and in Article 11 of this Protocol.

When in possession of this information, the Council shall draw up through its competent organs:

1. Plans of action for the application of the economic and financial sanctions against an aggressor State;

2. Plans of economic and financial co-operation between a State attacked and the different States assisting it;

and shall communicate these plans to the Members of the League and to the other signatory States.

ARTICLE 13

In view of the contingent military, naval and air sanctions provided for by Article 16 of the Covenant and by Article 11 of the present Protocol, the Council shall be entitled to receive undertakings from States determining in advance the military, naval and air forces which they would be able to bring into action immediately to ensure the fulfilment of the obligations in regard to sanctions which result from the Covenant and the present Protocol.

Furthermore, as soon as the Council has called upon the signatory States to apply sanctions, as provided in the last paragraph of Article 10 above, the said States may, in accordance with any agreements which they may previously have concluded, bring to the assistance of a particular State, which is the victim of aggression, their military, naval and air forces.

The agreements mentioned in the preceding paragraph shall be registered and published by the Secretariat of the League of Nations. They shall remain open to all States Members of the League which may desire to accede thereto.

ARTICLE 14

The Council shall alone be competent to declare that the application of sanctions shall cease and normal conditions be reestablished.

ARTICLE 15

In conformity with the spirit of the present Protocol, the signatory States agree that the whole cost of any military, naval or air operations undertaken for the repression of an aggression under the terms of the Protocol, and reparation for all losses suffered by individuals whether civilians or combatants, and for all material damage caused by the operations of both sides, shall be borne by the aggressor State up to the extreme limit of its capacity.

Nevertheless, in view of Article 10 of the Covenant, neither the territorial integrity nor the political independence of the aggressor State shall in any case be affected as the result of the applications of the sanctions mentioned in the present Protocol.

ARTICLE 16

The signatory States agree that in the event of a dispute between one or more of them and one or more States which have not signed the present Protocol and are not Members of the League of Nations, such non-Member States shall be invited, on the conditions contemplated in Article 17 of the Covenant, to submit, for the purpose of a pacific settlement, to the obligations accepted by the States signatories of the present Protocol.

If the State so invited, having refused to accept the said conditions and obligations, resorts to war against a signatory State, the provisions of Article 16 of the Covenant, as defined by the present Protocol, shall be applicable against it.

ARTICLE 17

The signatory States undertake to participate in an International Conference for the Reduction of Armaments which shall be convened by the Council and shall meet at Geneva on Monday, June 15th, 1925. All other States, whether Members of the League or not, shall be invited to this Conference.

In preparation for the convening of the Conference, the Council shall draw up with due regard to the undertakings contained in Articles 11 and 13 of the present Protocol a general programme for the reduction and limitation of armaments, which shall be laid before the Conference and which shall be communicated to the Governments at the earliest possible date, and at the latest three months before the Conference meets.

If by May 1st, 1925, ratifications have not been deposited by at least a majority of the permanent Members of the Council and ten other Members of the League, the Secretary-General of the League shall immediately consult the Council as to whether he shall cancel the invitations or merely adjourn the Conference until a sufficient number of ratifications have been deposited.

ARTICLE 18

Wherever mention is made in Article 10, or in any other provision of the present Protocol, of a decision of the Council, this shall be understood in the sense of Article 15 of the Covenant, namely that the votes of the representatives of the parties to the dispute shall not be counted when reckoning unanimity or the necessary majority.

ARTICLE 19

Except as expressly provided by its terms, the present Protocol shall not affect in any way the rights and obligations of Members of the League as determined by the Covenant.

ARTICLE 20

Any dispute as to the interpretation of the present Protocol shall be submitted to the Permanent Court of International Justice.

ARTICLE 21

The present Protocol, of which the French and English texts are both authentic, shall be ratified.

The deposit of ratification shall be made at the Secretariat of the League of Nations as soon as possible.

States of which the seat of government is outside Europe will be entitled merely to inform the Secretariat of the League of Nations that their ratification has been given; in that case, they must transmit the instrument of ratification as soon as possible.

So soon as the majority of the permanent Members of the Council and ten other Members of the League have deposited or have effected their ratifications, a procès-verbal to that effect shall be drawn up by the Secretariat.

After the said procès-verbal has been drawn up, the Protocol shall come into force as soon as the plan for the reduction of armaments has been adopted by the Conference provided for in Article 17.

If within such period after the adoption of the plan for the reduction of armaments as shall be fixed by the said Conference, the plan has not been carried out, the Council shall make a declaration to that effect; this declaration shall render the present Protocol null and void.

The grounds on which the Council may declare that the plan drawn up by the International Conference for the Reduction of Armaments has not been carried out, and that in consequence the present Protocol has been rendered null and void, shall be laid down by the Conference itself.

A signatory State which, after the expiration of the period fixed by the Conference, fails to comply with the plan adopted by the Conference, shall not be admitted to benefit by the provisions of the present Protocol.

In faith whereof the undersigned, duly authorised for this purpose, have signed the present Protocol.

DONE at Geneva, on the   day of October, Nineteen hundred and twenty-four, in a single copy, which will be kept in the archives of the Secretariat of the League and registered by it on the date of its coming into force.[1]

[1]*League of Nations Document,* C. 708. 1924. ix (C.C.O.I.).

PACIFIC SETTLEMENT OF INTERNATIONAL
DISPUTES, GENERAL ACT (1928)

Chapter I. Conciliation

ARTICLE 1

Disputes of every kind between two or more parties to the present General Act which it has not been possible to settle by diplomacy shall, subject to such reservations as may be made under Article 39, be submitted, under the conditions laid down in the present Chapter, to the procedure of conciliation.

ARTICLE 2

The disputes referred to in the preceding article shall be submitted to a permanent or special Conciliation Commission constituted by the parties to the dispute.

ARTICLE 3

On a request to that effect being made by one of the Contracting Parties to another party, a permanent Conciliation Commission shall be constituted within a period of six months.

ARTICLE 4

Unless the parties concerned agree otherwise, the Conciliation Commission shall be constituted as follows:

1. The Commission shall be composed of five members. The parties shall each nominate one commissioner, who may be chosen from among their respective nationals. The three other commissioners shall be appointed by agreement from among the nationals of third Powers. These three commissioners must be of different nationalities and must not be habitually resident in the territory nor be in the service of the parties. The parties shall appoint the President of the Commission from among them.

2. The commissioners shall be appointed for three years. They

shall be re-eligible. The commissioners appointed jointly may be replaced during the course of their mandate by agreement between the parties. Either party may, however, at any time replace a commissioner whom it has appointed. Even if replaced, the commissioners shall continue to exercise their functions until the termination of the work in hand.

3. Vacancies which may occur as a result of death, resignation or any other cause shall be filled within the shortest possible time in the manner fixed for the nominations.

ARTICLE 5

If, when a dispute arises, no permanent Conciliation Commission appointed by the parties is in existence, a special commission shall be constituted for the examination of the dispute within a period of three months from the date at which a request to that effect is made by one of the parties to the other party. The necessary appointments shall be made in the manner laid down in the preceding article, unless the parties decide otherwise.

ARTICLE 6

1. If the appointment of the commissioners to be designated jointly is not made within the periods provided for in Articles 3 and 5, the making of the necessary appointments shall be entrusted to a third Power, chosen by agreement between the parties, or on request of the parties, to the Acting President of the Council of the League of Nations.

2. If no agreement is reached on either of these procedures, each party shall designate a different Power, and the appointment shall be made in concert by the Powers thus chosen.

3. If, within a period of three months, the two Powers have been unable to reach an agreement, each of them shall submit a number of candidates equal to the number of members to be appointed. It shall then be decided by lot which of the candidates thus designated shall be appointed.

ARTICLE 7

1. Disputes shall be brought before the Conciliation Commission by means of an application addressed to the President by the two parties acting in agreement, or in default thereof by one or other of the parties.

2. The application, after giving a summary account of the subject of the dispute, shall contain the invitation to the Commission to take all necessary measures with a view to arriving at an amicable solution.

3. If the application emanates from only one of the parties, the other party shall, without delay, be notified by it.

Article 8

1. Within fifteen days from the date on which a dispute has been brought by one of the parties before a permanent Conciliation Commission, either party may replace its own commissioner, for the examination of the particular dispute, by a person possessing special competence in the matter.

2. The party making use of this right shall immediately notify the other party; the latter shall, in such case, be entitled to take similar action within fifteen days from the date on which it received the notification.

Article 9

1. In the absence of agreement to the contrary between the parties, the Conciliation Commission shall meet at the seat of the League of Nations, or at some other place selected by its President.

2. The Commission may in all circumstances request the Secretary-General of the League of Nations to afford it his assistance.

Article 10

The work of the Conciliation Commission shall not be conducted in public unless a decision to that effect is taken by the Commission with the consent of the parties.

Article 11

1. In the absence of agreement to the contrary between the parties, the Conciliation Commission shall lay down its own procedure, which in any case must provide for both parties being heard. In regard to enquiries, the Commission, unless it decides unanimously to the contrary, shall act in accordance with the provisions of Part III of the Hague Convention of October 18th, 1907, for the Pacific Settlement of International Disputes.

2. The parties shall be represented before the Conciliation Commission by agents, whose duty shall be to act as intermediaries

between them and the Commission; they may, moreover, be assisted by counsel and experts appointed by them for that purpose and may request that all persons whose evidence appears to them desirable shall be heard.

3. The Commission, for its part, shall be entitled to request oral explanations from the agents, counsel and experts of both parties, as well as from all persons it may think desirable to summon with the consent of their Governments.

ARTICLE 12

In the absence of agreement to the contrary between the parties, the decisions of the Conciliation Commission shall be taken by a majority vote, and the Commission may only take decisions on the substance of the dispute if all its members are present.

ARTICLE 13

The parties undertake to facilitate the work of the Conciliation Commission, and particularly to supply it to the greatest possible extent with all relevant documents and information, as well as to use the means at their disposal to allow it to proceed in their territory, and in accordance with their law, to the summoning and hearing of witnesses or experts and to visit the localities in question.

ARTICLE 14

1. During the proceedings of the Commission, each of the commissioners shall receive emoluments the amount of which shall be fixed by agreement between the parties, each of which shall contribute an equal share.

2. The general expenses arising out of the working of the Commission shall be divided in the same manner.

ARTICLE 15

1. The task of the Conciliation Commission shall be to elucidate the questions in dispute, to collect with that object all necessary information by means of enquiry or otherwise, and to endeavour to bring the parties to an agreement. It may, after the case has been examined, inform the parties of the terms of settlement which seem suitable to it, and lay down the period within which they are to make their decision.

2. At the close of its proceedings, the Commission shall draw up

a proces-verbal stating, as the case may be, either that the parties have come to an agreement and, if need arises, the terms of the agreement, or that it has been impossible to effect a settlement. No mention shall be made in the proces-verbal of whether the Commission's decisions were taken unanimously or by a majority vote.

3. The proceedings of the Commission must, unless the parties otherwise agree, be terminated within six months from the date on which the Commission shall have been given cognisance of the dispute.

ARTICLE 16

The Commission's proces-verbal shall be communicated without delay to the parties. The parties shall decide whether it shall be published.

Chapter II. Judicial Settlement

ARTICLE 17

All disputes with regard to which the parties are in conflict as to their respective rights shall, subject to any reservations which may be made under Article 39, be submitted for decision to the Permanent Court of International Justice, unless the parties agree, in the manner hereinafter provided, to have resort to an arbitral tribunal.

It is understood that the disputes referred to above include in particular those mentioned in Article 36 of the Statute of the Permanent Court of International Justice.

ARTICLE 18

If the parties agree to submit the disputes mentioned in the preceding article to an arbitral tribunal, they shall draw up a special agreement, the provisions of the Hague Convention of October 18th, 1907, for the Pacific Settlement of International Disputes shall apply so far as is necessary. If nothing is laid down in the special agreement as to the rules regarding the substance of the dispute to be followed by the arbitrators, the tribunal shall apply the substantive rules enumerated in Article 38 of the Statute of the Permanent Court of International Justice.

ARTICLE 19

If the parties fail to agree concerning the special agreement referred to in the preceding article, or fail to appoint arbitrators, either party shall be at liberty, after giving three months' notice, to bring the dispute by an application direct before the Permanent Court of International Justice.

ARTICLE 20

1. Notwithstanding the provisions of Article 1, disputes of the kind referred to in Article 17 arising between parties who have acceded to the obligations contained in the present chapter shall only be subject to the procedure of conciliation if the parties so agree.

2. The obligation to resort to the procedure of conciliation remains applicable to disputes which are excluded from judicial settlement only by the operation of reservations under the provisions of Article 39.

3. In the event of recourse to and failure of conciliation, neither party may bring the dispute before the Permanent Court of International Justice or call for the constitution of the Arbitral Tribunal referred to in Article 18 before the expiration of one month from the termination of the proceedings of the Conciliation Commission.

Chapter III. Arbitration

ARTICLE 21

Any dispute not of the kind referred to in Article 17 which does not, within the month following the termination of the work of the Conciliation Commission provided for in Chapter I, form the object of an agreement between the parties, may, subject to such reservations as may be made under Article 39, be brought before an arbitral tribunal which, unless the parties otherwise agree, shall be constituted in the manner set out below.

ARTICLE 22

The Arbitral Tribunal shall consist of five members. The parties shall each nominate one member, who may be chosen from among their respective nationals. The two other arbitrators and the Chairman shall be chosen by common agreement from among the nationals of third Powers. They must be of different nationalities and must not be habitually resident in the territory nor be in the service of the parties.

ARTICLE 23

1. If the appointment of the members of the Arbitral Tribunal is not made within a period of three months from the date on which one of the parties requested the other party to constitute an arbitral tribunal, a third Power, chosen by agreement between the parties, shall be requested to make the necessary appointments.

2. If no agreement is reached on this point, each party shall designate a different Power, and the appointments shall be made in concert by the Powers thus chosen.

3. If, within a period of three months, the two Powers so chosen have been unable to reach an agreement, the necessary appointments shall be made by the President of the Permanent Court of International Justice. If the latter is prevented from acting or is a subject of one of the parties, the nomination shall be made by the Vice-President. If the latter is prevented from acting or is a subject of one of the parties, the appointments shall be made by the oldest member of the Court who is not a subject of either party.

ARTICLE 24

Vacancies which may occur as a result of death, resignation or any other cause shall be filled within the shortest possible time in the manner fixed for the nominations.

ARTICLE 25

The parties shall draw up a special agreement determining the subject of the disputes and the details of procedure.

ARTICLE 26

In the absence of sufficient particulars in the special agreement regarding the matters referred to in the preceding article, the provisions of the Hague Convention of October 18th, 1907, for the Pacific Settlement of International Disputes shall apply so far as is necessary.

ARTICLE 27

Failing the conclusion of a special agreement within a period of three months from the date on which the Tribunal was constituted, the dispute may be brought before the Tribunal by an application by one or other party.

ARTICLE 28

If nothing is laid down in the special agreement or no special agreement has been made, the Tribunal shall apply the rules in regard to the substance of the dispute enumerated in Article 38 of the Statute of the Permanent Court of International Justice. In so far as there exists no such rule applicable to the dispute, the Tribunal shall decide *ex aequo et bono*.

Chapter IV. General Provisions

ARTICLE 29

1. Disputes for the settlement of which a special procedure is laid down in other conventions in force between the parties to the dispute shall be settled in conformity with the provisions of those conventions.

2. The present General Act shall not affect any agreements in force by which conciliation procedure is established between the parties or they are bound by obligations to resort to arbitration or judicial settlement which ensure the settlement of the dispute. If, however, these agreements provide only for a procedure of conciliation, after such procedure has been followed without result, the provisions of the present General Act concerning judicial settlement or arbitration shall be applied in so far as the parties have acceded thereto.

ARTICLE 30

If a party brings before a Conciliation Commission a dispute which the other party, relying on conventions in force between the parties, has submitted to the Permanent Court of International Justice or an Arbitral Tribunal, the Commission shall defer consideration of the dispute until the Court or the Arbitral Tribunal has pronounced upon the conflict of competence. The same rule shall apply if the Court or the Tribunal is seized of the case by one of the parties during the conciliation proceedings.

ARTICLE 31

1. In the case of a dispute the occasion of which, according to the municipal law of one of the parties, falls within the competence of its judicial or administrative authorities, the party in question may

object to the matter in dispute being submitted for settlement by the different methods laid down in the present General Act until a decision with final effect has been pronounced, within a reasonable time, by the competent authority.

2. In such a case, the party which desires to resort to the procedures laid down in the present General Act must notify the other party of its intention within a period of one year from the date of the aforementioned decision.

ARTICLE 32

If, in a judicial sentence or arbitral award, it is declared that a judgment, or a measure enjoined by a court of law or other authority of one of the parties to the dispute, is wholly or in part contrary to international law, and if the constitutional law of that party does not permit or only partially permits the consequences of the judgment or measure in question to be annulled, the parties agree that the judicial sentence or arbitral award shall grant the injured party equitable satisfaction.

ARTICLE 33

1. In all cases where a dispute forms the object of arbitration or judicial proceedings, and particularly if the question on which the parties differ arises out of acts already committed or on the point of being committed, the Permanent Court of International Justice, acting in accordance with Article 41 of its Statute, or the Arbitral Tribunal, shall lay down within the shortest possible time the provisional measures to be adopted. The parties to the dispute shall be bound to accept such measures.

2. If the dispute is brought before a Conciliation Commission, the latter may recommend to the parties the adoption of such provisional measures as it considers suitable.

3. The parties undertake to abstain from all measures likely to react prejudicially upon the execution of the judicial or arbitral decision or upon the arrangements proposed by the Conciliation Commission and, in general, to abstain from any sort of action whatsoever which may aggravate or extend the dispute.

ARTICLE 34

Should a dispute arise between more than two parties to the

present General Act, the following rules shall be observed for the application of the forms of procedure described in the foregoing provisions:

(a) In the case of conciliation procedure, a special commission shall invariably be constituted. The composition of such commission shall differ according as the parties all have separate interests or as two or more of their number act together.

In the former case, the parties shall each appoint one commissioner and shall jointly appoint commissioners nationals of third Powers not parties to the dispute, whose number shall always exceed by one the number of commissioners appointed separately by the parties.

In the second case, the parties who act together shall appoint their commissioner jointly by agreement between themselves and shall combine with the other party or parties in appointing third commissioners.

In either event, the parties, unless they agree otherwise, shall apply Article 5 and the following articles of the present Act, so far as they are compatible with the provisions of the present article.

(b) In the case of judicial procedure, the Statute of the Permanent Court of International Justice shall apply.

(c) In the case of arbitral procedure, if agreement is not secured as to the composition of the tribunal, in the case of the disputes mentioned in Article 17 each party shall have the right, by means of an application, to submit the dispute to the Permanent Court of International Justice; in the case of the disputes mentioned in Article 21, the above Article 22 and following articles shall apply, but each party having separate interests shall appoint one arbitrator and the number of arbitrators separately appointed by the parties to the dispute shall always be one less than that of the other arbitrators.

ARTICLE 35

1. The present General Act shall be applicable as between the parties thereto, even though a third Power, whether a party to the Act or not, has an interest in the dispute.

2. In conciliation procedure, the parties may agree to invite such third Power to intervene.

ARTICLE 36

1. In judicial or arbitral procedure, if a third Power should consider that it has an interest of a legal nature which may be affected by the decision in case, it may submit to the Permanent Court of International Justice or to the arbitral tribunal a request to intervene as a third Party.

2. It will be for the Court or the tribunal to decide upon this request.

ARTICLE 37

1. Whenever the construction of a convention to which States other than those concerned in the case are parties is in question, the Registrar of the Permanent Court of International Justice or the arbitral tribunal shall notify all such States forthwith.

2. Every State so notified has the right to intervene in the proceedings; but, if it uses this right, the construction given by the decision will be binding upon it.

ARTICLE 38

Accessions to the present General Act may extend:

A. Either to all the provisions of the Act (Chapters I, II, III and IV);

B. Or to those provisions only which relate to conciliation and judicial settlement (Chapters I and II), together with the general provisions dealing with these procedures (Chapter IV);

C. Or to those provisions only which relate to conciliation (Chapter I), together with the General Provisions concerning that procedure (Chapter IV).

The Contracting Parties may benefit by the accessions of other parties only in so far as they have themselves assumed the same obligations.

ARTICLE 39

1. In addition to the power given in the preceding Article, a party, in acceding to the present General Act, may make his acceptance conditional upon the reservations exhaustively enumerated in the following paragraph. These reservations must be indicated at the time of accession.

2. These reservations may be such as to exclude from the procedure described in the present Act:

(a) Disputes arising out of facts prior to the accession either of the party making the reservation or of any other party with whom the said party may have a dispute;

(b) Disputes concerning questions which by international law are solely within the domestic jurisdiction of States;

(c) Disputes concerning particular cases or clearly specified subject-matters, such as territorial status, or disputes falling within clearly defined categories.

3. If one of the parties to a dispute has made a reservation, the other parties may enforce the same reservation in regard to that party.

4. In the case of parties who have acceded to the provisions of the present General Act relating to judicial settlement or to arbitration, such reservations as they may have made shall, unless otherwise expressly stated, be deemed not to apply to the procedure of conciliation.

ARTICLE 40

A party whose accession has been only partial, or was made subject to reservations, may at any moment, by means of a simple declaration, either extend the scope of his accession or abandon all or part of his reservations.

ARTICLE 41

Disputes relating to the interpretation or application of the present General Act, including those concerning the classification of disputes and the scope of reservations, shall be submitted to the Permanent Court of International Justice.

ARTICLE 42

The present General Act, of which the French and English texts shall both be authentic, shall bear the date of the 26th of September, 1928.

ARTICLE 43

1. The present General Act shall be open to accession by all the Heads of States or other competent authorities of the Members of the League of Nations and the non-Member States to which the

Council of the League of Nations has communicated a copy for this purpose.

2. The instruments of accession and the additional declarations provided for by Article 40 shall be transmitted to the Secretary-General of the League of Nations, who shall notify their receipt to all the Members of the League and to the non-Member States referred to in the preceding paragraph.

3. The Secretary-General of the League of Nations shall draw up three lists, denominated respectively by the letters A, B and C, corresponding to the three forms of accession to the present Act provided for in Article 38, in which shall be shown the accessions and additional declarations of the Contracting Parties. These lists, which shall be continually kept up to date, shall be published in the annual report presented to the Assembly of the League of Nations by the Secretary-General.

Article 44

1. The present General Act shall come into force on the ninetieth day following the receipt by the Secretary-General of the League of Nations of the accession of not less than two Contracting Parties.

2. Accessions received after the entry into force of the Act, in accordance with the previous paragraph, shall become effective as from the ninetieth day following the date of receipt by the Secretary-General of the League of Nations. The same rule shall apply to the additional declarations provided for by Article 40.

Article 45

1. The present General Act shall be concluded for a period of five years, dating from its entry into force.

2. It shall remain in force for further successive periods of five years in the case of Contracting Parties which do not denounce it at least six months before the expiration of the current period.

3. Denunciation shall be effected by a written notification addressed to the Secretary-General of the League of Nations, who shall inform all the Members of the League and the non-Member States referred to in Article 43.

4. A denunciation may be partial only, or may consist in notification of reservations not previously made.

5. Notwithstanding denunciation by one of the Contracting Parties concerned in a dispute, all proceedings pending at the expiration of the current period of the General Act shall be duly completed.

ARTICLE 46

A copy of the present General Act, signed by the President of the Assembly and by the Secretary-General of the League of Nations, shall be deposited in the archives of the Secretariat; a certified true copy shall be delivered by the Secretary-General to all the Members of the League of Nations and to the non-Member States indicated by the Council of the League of Nations.

ARTICLE 47

The present General Act shall be registered by the Secretary-General of the League of Nations on the date of its entry into force.

September 26, 1928.[1]

[1]*League of Nations Document*, C. 537. M. 164. 1928. IX.

CONVENTION TO IMPROVE THE MEANS
OF PREVENTING WAR (1931)

ARTICLE 1. The High Contracting Parties undertake, in the event of a dispute arising between them and being brought before the Council of the League of Nations, to accept and apply the conservatory measures of a non-military nature relating to the substance of the dispute which the Council, acting in accordance with the powers conferred upon it by the Covenant of the League of Nations, may recommend with a view to preventing the aggravation of the dispute.

The Council shall fix the period of duration of these conservatory measures. It may extend this period should circumstances render it necessary.

ART. 2. If, in circumstances which, in the Council's opinion, do not create a state of war between the Powers at issue which are parties to the present Convention, the forces of one of those Powers enter the territory or territorial waters of the other or a zone demilitarised in virtue of international agreements, or fly over them, the Council may prescribe measures to ensure their evacuation by those forces. The High Contracting Parties undertake to carry out without delay the measures so prescribed, without prejudice to the other powers vested in the Council under Article II of the Covenant.

ART. 3. If the circumstances referred to in Article 2 have arisen, or if, in the event of a threat of war, special conditions, and in particular the possibilities of contact between the forces of the parties to the dispute, render it necessary, the Council may fix lines which must not be passed by their land, naval or air forces and, where necessary in order to avoid incidents, by their civil aircraft. The High Contracting Parties undertake to comply with the Council's recommendations in this matter.

The lines referred to in the previous paragraph shall, if possible, be fixed by agreement with the parties at issue.

Failing such agreement, the Council shall fix the lines with the consent of the party whose forces are affected, provided always that this does not involve the withdrawal of the forces further back than the exterior lines of the defence organisations existing on the frontier of the High Contracting Parties concerned at the time when the Council of the League of Nations takes its decision, and that the lines do not involve the abandonment of any other work, position or line of communication essential to the security or the supplies of the party concerned.

It shall, in every case, rest with the Council to determine the period within which the said lines shall be fixed under the conditions specified above.

The High Contracting Parties further agree to give strict orders to the commanders of their forces, if the Council so recommends, to take all necessary precautions to avoid incidents.

ART. 4. The Council shall, if it thinks fit, or if one of the parties at issue so requests before the Council has reached any of the decisions referred to in Articles 2 and 3, appoint commissioners for the sole purpose of verifying on the spot the execution of the conservatory measures of a military character recommended by the Council under the conditions specified in Articles 2 and 3.

When regulating the execution of the measures it has prescribed, the Council shall, at the reasoned request of a High Contracting Party which is a party to the dispute, cause that execution to coincide with the arrival of the commissioners on the spot, so far as it may think necessary.

The High Contracting Parties undertake to afford these commissioners every facility for the performance of their duties.

The commissioners may not make a more extensive inspection than is necessary to enable them to carry out the duty defined in paragraph 1. Nor may they make any inspection of a naval or air base, nor may they inspect military works or establishments for any purpose other than to verify the withdrawal of the forces.

The rules to be followed for the composition and working of

commissions of inspection shall be embodied in executive regulations which shall be prepared by the competent organs of the League of Nations so as to enter into force at the same time as the present Convention.

ART. 5. If any violation of the measures defined in Articles 2 and 3 is noted by the Council and continues in spite of its injunctions, the Council shall consider what means of all kinds are necessary to ensure the execution of the present Convention.

Should war break out as a consequence of this violation, such violation shall be regarded by the High Contracting Parties as prima facie evidence that the party guilty thereof has resorted to war within the meaning of Article 16 of the Covenant.

ART. 6. The High Contracting Parties undertake to provide, by the means at their disposal, such publicity as the Council may think fit for its proceedings, decisions and recommendations when a dispute is brought before it in the cases contemplated by the present Convention.

ART. 7. In the cases referred to in Articles 1, 2, 3, 4, 5, and 6, the Council's decisions and recommendations shall, except as otherwise provided in those articles, be binding for the purposes of the present Convention, provided that they are concurred in by all the Members voting other than the parties to the dispute.

ART. 8. The provisions of the present Convention shall only apply as between the High Contracting Parties.

ART. 9. The present Convention may not be interpreted as restricting the task or the powers of the Council of the League of Nations as laid down in the Covenant.

Nor should it affect the right of free passage through the Suez Canal provided for in the Convention on the Free Navigation of the Suez Maritime Canal signed at Constantinople on October 29th, 1888.

ART. 10. The present Convention shall remain open until February 2nd, 1932, for signatures on behalf of any Member of the League of Nations or of any non-member State to which the Council of the League of Nations has communicated a copy of the Convention for this purpose.

Art. 11. The present Convention is subject to ratification. Ratifications shall be deposited with the Secretariat of the League of Nations.

The Secretary-General shall give notice of the deposit of each ratification to the Members of the League of Nations and to the non-member States mentioned in Article 10, indicating the date of its deposit.

Art. 12. As from February 3rd, 1932, any Member of the League of Nations and any non-member State mentioned in Article 10 on whose behalf the Convention has not been signed before that date may accede thereto.

Accession shall be effected by an instrument deposited with the Secretariat of the League of Nations. The Secretary-General of the League of Nations shall give notice of each accession to the Members of the League of Nations and to the non-member States mentioned in Article 10, indicating the date of the deposit of the instrument.

Art. 13. A *procès-verbal* shall be drawn up by the Secretary-General of the League of Nations as soon as ratifications or accessions on behalf of ten Members of the League of Nations or non-member States have been deposited.

A certified copy of this *procès-verbal* shall be sent by the Secretary-General of the League of Nations to each Member of the League of Nations and to each non-member State mentioned in Article 10.

Art. 14. The present Convention shall be registered by the Secretary-General of the League of Nations ninety days after the date mentioned in Article 13. It will then enter into force as regards all Members of the League of Nations or non-member States on whose behalf ratifications or accessions have been deposited on the date of the *procès-verbal*.

As regards any Member of the League or non-member State on whose behalf a ratification or accession is subsequently deposited, the Convention shall enter into force on the ninetieth day after the date of the deposit of a ratification or accession on its behalf.

Each of the High Contracting Parties shall have the right to inform the Secretary-General of the League of Nations at the moment of the deposit of his ratification or of the notification of his accession, to the exclusion of all other reservations, that he makes the entry into force of the Convention, in so far as he is concerned, conditional on ratification or accession on behalf of certain countries named by him.

ART. 15. The present Convention may not be denounced before the expiration of five years from its coming into force in accordance with Article 14.

Denunciation shall be effected by a notification in writing addressed to the Secretary-General of the League of Nations, who shall inform all Members of the League of Nations and the non-member States mentioned in Article 10. Each denunciation shall take effect one year after the receipt by the Secretary-General of the notification, but only as regards the High Contracting Party on whose behalf it has been notified.

ART. 16. The French and English texts of the present Convention shall both be authoritative.

IN FAITH WHEREOF the above-mentioned Plenipotentiaries have signed the present Convention.

Done at Geneva, on the twenty-sixth day of September, one thousand nine hundred and thirty-one, in a single copy, which shall be deposited in the archives of the Secretariat of the League of Nations, and of which certified true copies shall be transmitted by the Secretary-General to all the Members of the League of Nations and to any non-member State to which the Council of the League of Nations has decided to communicate a copy of the present Convention, in accordance with Article 10.[1]

[1]League of Nations, Conference for the Reduction and Limitation of Armaments, *Conference Documents* (IX Disarmament. 1935. IX. 4), II, p. 313.

REGULATIONS UNDER ARTICLE 4 OF THE CONVENTION TO IMPROVE THE MEANS OF PREVENTING WAR

CHAPTER I

Constitution of Commissions of Inspection

ARTICLE 1. When there is occasion to constitute a Commission of Inspection, the commissioners shall be appointed by the Council of the League of Nations with the approval of the States of which such experts are nationals.

The commissioners may not be nationals of the parties to the dispute.

ART. 2. The Council may request the Permanent Advisory Commission for Military, Naval and Air Questions to submit to it, according to the circumstances and the nature of the conservatory measures contemplated, proposals in regard to the exact composition of the Commission, its organisation and its working.

ART. 3. Unless otherwise decided by the Council, the Commission of Inspection shall include the same number of commissioners of each nationality represented on the commission.

ART. 4. The Council shall appoint the President of the Commission. The latter shall organise the work of the Commission subject to the provisions of the Convention and of the present regulations.

ART. 5. The Commission may be divided into several sections. Each section shall consist of not less than three members. These shall be of different nationalities.

ART. 6. If a section consists entirely of officers, the senior member of the highest rank shall be President of the section.

If a section consists of both civilians and officers, its President shall be appointed by the President of the Commission. However, the President of the Commission may not appoint an officer other than the senior member of the highest rank.

If there are several sections, their Presidents shall as far as possible be of different nationalities.

CHAPTER II
Work of the Commissions

ART. 7. The rôle of the Commission of Inspection is defined and limited by Article 4 of the Convention (first and fourth paragraphs). The Commission shall also comply with the detailed instructions it may have received from the Council of the League of Nations.

ART. 8. In the event of the application of Article 2 of the Convention, the commissioners shall have, subject to the provisions contained in the fourth paragraph of Article 4 of the Convention, the right to visit any point to which they may have to proceed in execution of their mission and to remain there as long as may be necessary for the purpose of verifying on the spot the execution of the conservatory measures recommended by the Council.

In the event of the application of Article 3 of the Convention, the commissioners shall, for the performance of the mission entrusted to them by the Council, have the right to move about freely and to remain within the zone between the lines fixed by the Council in accordance with the said article. This right shall be guaranteed to them even if hostilities not creating a state of war should have occurred.

On land, if the said zones determined with the consent of the parties concerned under the conditions laid down in the second paragraph of Article 3 include military establishments, the commissioners shall have the right to enter and remain in those establishments for the performance of their mission.

On sea, in the case of warships of one of the parties being authorised to pass through one of the above-mentioned zones, in order to ensure the necessary communications between the various territories of the said party, the President of the Commission may depute commissioners to go on board these warships.

As regards the supervision of the movements of aircraft, the commissioners shall have the right to establish lookout posts either at the frontiers or in the zones referred to in the second paragraph of this article. If the Council has not forbidden civil aircraft to approach the frontiers or the intermediate zone, the commissioners shall have the right to fix compulsory crossing points for civil aircraft. Should the Commission not have at its disposal the means required for supervising night flying this may be prohibited at the frontiers or in the said zones to all aircraft by the President of the Commission.

If one of the parties so requests, the President of the Commission shall depute one or more commissioners to accompany any land, sea or air forces of the said party which, moving near one of the above-mentioned zones, might wish to prove that they have not entered that zone.

Subject to arrangements to be concluded with the parties, enabling the commissioners to make themselves known, they shall comply as far as possible with the rules of international law on the employment of envoys, in so far as those rules do not impede the performance of their mission.

ART. 9. The commissioners shall enjoy all diplomatic privileges and immunities.

They shall be provided as soon as possible, in addition to diplomatic passports or visas, with identity papers drawn up by the Secretary-General of the League of Nations in the name of the Council indicating the official status of the holder and the mission entrusted to him.

CHAPTER III

Facilities to Be Accorded to Commissions of Inspection by the Parties to the Dispute

ART. 10. The Governments parties to the Convention to which the Council shall have notified the dispatch of a Commission of Inspection shall take the necessary measures to enable the commissioners to discharge their duties. They shall see that the public authorities and the population place no obstacle of any kind in the way of the work of the Commission. They shall give the latter all assistance in their power in order to facilitate the accomplishment of its mission. They shall, more particularly, appoint one or more officials who shall be at the constant disposal of the Commission. Such officials shall be provided with written instructions giving them full powers to call for the assistance of the civil and military authorities.

During the execution of their mission, the commissioners may not refuse the company of officials of the State party to the dispute in whose territory their mission is being performed.

ART. 11. The Governments parties to the Convention shall give instructions to the responsible authorities, with a view to ensuring that transport of persons belonging to the Commissions and communications of all kinds between the Commissions and the Council of the League of Nations shall be effected as rapidly as possible.

ART. 12. The Governments parties to the dispute shall give instructions to the responsible authorities to offer the commissioners any protection that may be asked for by them.

ART. 13. The Governments parties to the dispute shall on their respective territories provide the Commission with all facilities for transport and accommodation that might reasonably be requested.

The expenses of transport and accommodation shall be defrayed by the commissioners.

ART. 14. The Governments parties to the dispute shall send to the Council of the League of Nations and to the President of the Commission a copy of the orders, powers and instructions that they may have given in conformity with the provisions of the present chapter.

CHAPTER IV
Reports

ART. 15. The President shall keep the Council informed of the activities of the Commission of Inspection. He shall in particular inform the Council immediately of any infraction of the conservatory measures recommended which might be committed by the parties.

In order to permit the application of the provisions of the second paragraph of Article 4 of the Convention, the President of the Commission shall immediately inform the Council, under the conditions laid down in Article 11 of the present rules, of the arrival on the spot of the commissioners and of the precise time at which they will be in a position to perform their mission.

Should any difficulty arise between the Commission and the authorities of any one of the parties to the dispute, the President shall immediately inform the Council. Pending the decision by the Council, the President of the Commission shall take all necessary steps to enable the commissioners to continue their mission under the most effective conditions possible. The Government of the party concerned shall instruct its responsible authorities to assist the commissioners for this purpose on all points not directly affecting the difficulty in question.

ART. 16. On the conclusion of the mission, the President of the Commission shall submit to the Council of the League of Nations the Commission's report, and also, in the event of disagreement, any dissenting opinions.

CHAPTER V
Secretariat and Financial Provisions

ART. 17. Should the Council consider it necessary, a secretariat for the Commission shall be organised by the Secretary-General of the League of Nations. The members of that secretariat shall enjoy the same diplomatic privileges and immunities as the commissioners.

ART. 18. The allowance granted to the commissioners shall be fixed by the Council on the advice of the Secretary-General of the League of Nations, and shall be calculated on the basis of those generally given for similar missions. Unless otherwise decided by the Council, the expenses attaching to such Commissions shall be borne by the parties to the dispute.

ART. 19. The necessary funds shall be advanced to persons belonging to the Commissions by the Secretariat of the League of Nations, under conditions fixed by the Council in conformity with the regulations for the financial administration of the League of Nations.[1]

[1]League of Nations, Conference for Reduction and Limitation of Armaments, *Conference Documents* (IX. Disarmament. 1935. IX), II, p. 352.